ROBERT LOUIS STEVENSON

BY

SIDNEY DARK

HASKELL HOUSE PUBLISHERS LTD.
Publishers of Scarce Scholarly Books
NEW YORK, N. Y. 10012
1971

First Published 1931

HASKELL HOUSE PUBLISHERS LTD.
Publishers of Scarce Scholarly Books
280 LAFAYETTE STREET
NEW YORK. N. Y. 10012

Library of Congress Catalog Card Number: 76-173849

Standard Book Number 8383-1343-4

Printed in the United States of America

ALL of the books from which I have quoted are acknowledged in footnotes. I have to express my indebtedness to Messrs. Heinemann for permission to quote from the text and the introductions to the Tusitala edition of Stevenson's works, and it should be understood that it is the Tusitala edition to which I refer in the footnotes. I have also their permission to quote from Sir Edmund Gosse's essays. It would be impossible to write a study of Stevenson without frequent references to Sir Graham Balfour's official *Life*, and I am grateful to Messrs. Methuen for their permission to quote, as I am to Messrs. Edward Arnold & Co. for permission to quote from the late Sir Walter Raleigh's study.

CONTENTS

CHAPTER I

PRINCE CHARMING

NEVER has there been a generation so eager as this to destroy the gods of their fathers. "Victorianism" has become the last word of contempt. Taste in literature and art must vary from age to age, and is obviously influenced by the general attitude to life and by the generally accepted values. Sometimes to-day has been the obvious child of yesterday. Sometimes it is the reaction against yesterday. Always it is different. Our to-day is mightily different.

In my young manhood, not to appreciate George Meredith, in his poetry as well as in his fiction, was to be counted among the Philistines. Nowadays a reputation for culture depends on enthusiasm for Marcel Proust, D. H. Lawrence, and Mr. Aldous Huxley. A generation has arisen which finds its keenest aesthetic pleasure in the skilful description of a society in which men and women sin strenuously but without satisfaction.

This is not the place, though it would be an interesting study, to compare the realism of the twentieth century with the realism of the nineteenth. But it is inevitable that such a writer as

A

Robert Louis Stevenson, who was conspicuous in the revolt against the fundamentally untrue and therefore unrealistic realism of last century, should be neglected, if not despised, now that Mr. Aldous Huxley has become the model for the youngest writers to copy. In this, of course, Stevenson is not alone. Hardy is too sure of his place among the immortals to be altogether neglected, but who now acclaims the greatness of Meredith as Stevenson acclaimed it? So fine and sensitive a writer as Maurice Hewlett is little read. Conrad has passed from the perhaps exaggerated praise that was his while he lived to the period of depreciation that commonly follows over-praise. Certain of the older living writers of established reputations retain their publics, but their claim to greatness, unquestioned fifteen years ago, is now by no means generally admitted.

Writing of modern criticism, Professor George Saintsbury has said : " If it sometimes amuses itself with making, say, Socrates and Stevenson into ' myths,' the mythopœic faculty is notoriously strong in the young. . . . I know that Stevenson, and I think that Socrates, would have enjoyed being a ' myth ' immensely." [1]

The new realism is the direct result of the war. It is the result of the discovery that pomp and circumstance mean poisoned gas, murdered civilians, unemployment, and high taxes.

[1] *A Scrap Book* (Saintsbury), pp. 281-2.

To-day, men have grown pugnaciously self-conscious. The most intimate details of the individual life appear of such supreme importance that they must be discussed in the market-place and shouted from the housetop. A new morality is demanded for a new earth, and nobody who really matters believes either in an old or a new heaven. But all the truth is not told by the new realists, as it was not told by the old realists, and in the circumstances there may be some interest and perhaps some small value in the reconsideration of the achievement and character of a man who wrote romances and lived romantically. The world has come, not without reason, to regard the picturesque with suspicion! And Robert Louis Stevenson was nothing if not picturesque. The world, too, is cynically doubtful of the eulogies of friends. And Stevenson was loved by his friends. Much has been written of his life and his work, perhaps too much. Mr. E. F. Benson has declared that the actual bulk of the printed matter which his friends have written in record of their memories of him must easily exceed that of Boswell's *Life of Johnson*.[1] But Stevenson was the last man who could be accurately appraised by his friends. Few men can ever have so completely dazzled their friends as Stevenson dazzled his. Swinburne, Sir Edmund Gosse says, was practically alone among his contemporaries in regarding him

[1] *The Myth of R. L. S., London Mercury*, Nos. 69 and 70.

as having no talent. To Sir Edmund, however, who in his later life did not appear a man easily moved to enthusiasm, Stevenson was " the most unselfish and the most lovable of human beings," [1] and Sir Sidney Colvin has declared that " there seemed to be more vitality and fire of the spirit in him as he lay exhausted and speechless in bed than in an ordinary roomful of people in health." [2] Andrew Lang wrote : " I have known no man in whom pre-eminently manly virtues of kindness, courage, sympathy, generosity, helpfulness, were more beautifully conspicuous than in Mr. Stevenson, no man so much loved—it is not too strong a word—by so many and such various people.   He was as unique in character as in literary genius."[3]

The language of hyperbole may be sincere, but it is never convincing. I share Mr. Benson's doubt whether the complete and real Stevenson is to be discovered in the glowing tributes of Sir Edmund Gosse, Sir Sidney Colvin, and Andrew Lang, or in the panegyric of Miss Rosaline Masson. Stevenson had, with the rest of us, his many glaring faults.   The grave Sir Edmund protested that he could remember none of them.   Certainly Stevenson dazzled his friends almost as much as he dazzled himself.

It is not unreasonable, too, to question the

[1] *Critical Kit-Kats*, by Edmund Gosse, p. 302.
[2] *Letters*, vol. i., Introd., p. xxii.
[3] *Adventures Among Books*, by Andrew Lang, p. 51.

critical judgments of his work written by men who loved him so uncritically. Is there, for example, justification for Sir Edmund Gosse's description of him as " the most exquisite English writer of his generation." In another place, Sir Edmund has said that " it is from the point of view of its charm that the genius of Stevenson must be approached, and in this respect there was between himself and his books, his manners and his style, his practice and his theory, a very unusual harmony." [1] Sir Edmund himself admits that it was very difficult for any of Stevenson's friends rightly to gauge the purely literary significance of Stevenson's works.

It should be remembered, too, that in the last two decades of last century the English critic of letters was busy discovering masterpieces. And when a genius was discovered—this happened about once a week—the critic called on his friends to rejoice with him over that which he had found. One critic, generally also a creative writer, passed the buck to another equally versatile. It was the age of the persistent log-roller. I recall the lavish praise given by sober critics of the class of W. L. Courtney and William Archer to the plays of Stephen Phillips who, it was declared, possessed the genius of both Shakespeare and Milton. Now the Phillips plays are as dead as the bread-and-butter comedies of T. W.

[1] *Encyclopaedia Britannica.*

Robertson. Is it possible to justify to a later and
essentially unbelieving generation similar pæans
excited by the prose and verse of Robert Louis
Stevenson, bearing in mind the irresistible charm
of his personality, which was sufficient to make it
possible even for Henley to ignore for years the
Shorter Catechist whom he abhorred.

Was the man Stevenson, who struggled manfully all through his life against disease, who with
the body of a weakling lived the life of an adventurer, greater than the works of Stevenson the
writer ? " A high and simple courage shines
through all his writing," wrote Walter Raleigh.
But perhaps a higher courage shone through his
life. Mr. Chesterton thinks so, and in the obitu-
ary that Henley published in the *New Review*,
William Archer declared that Stevenson's books
were " but broken lights of him, and he in very
truth was more than they." If that be so, here
is a man worth knowing. " Within its limits, his
life was a masterpiece," wrote Mr. Archer. And
can any age afford to neglect the artist in life ?

How is he to be discovered ? I agree with Mr.
Benson, not in the effusive eulogies of his friends.
Certainly not in " the exasperated scream " of
W. E. Henley. Perhaps in his books and in his
letters. There indeed I have tried to find him.
I have one qualification for the search, for with
Mr. Humbert Wolfe I have for Stevenson " a
quite irrevocable affection."

CHAPTER II

THE TROUBLED COVENANTER

THE two facts of outstanding importance concerning Robert Louis Stevenson are that he was a Scotsman, and that he was a sick man from his boyhood.

National temperamental differences are commonly exaggerated, but they are not to be ignored if misunderstanding is to be avoided. One reason for the constant trouble between the English and the Irish was the English conviction that the Irish are merely rather irresponsible English, with an unpleasant sense of humour and none of the moral fibre for which the English like to believe that they are distinguished. Thirty years ago, the suggestion that the Irish are, in all fundamentals, a people as apart from the English as the French, and far more apart than the Germans—this is as true of the black Protestant of Belfast as of the Catholic of County Cork—was ridiculed in England, and the Nationalist slogan, "Ireland a nation," was regarded as a silly joke. The Englishman always finds it difficult to believe that everybody who speaks English, even when he speaks it with a strange accent, is not an Englishman, and this accounts for the common English impatience with the United States. Geographically and spiritually the Middle West is much farther away from London than the Near East. Edinburgh is separated from England only by a few miles, and there are many points of similarity between the English and the Scottish characters. None the less, the one thing certain of a Scotsman is that he is not an Englishman.

Stevenson has himself recorded that in his foreign travels he was often taken for a Frenchman, and once for a Pole, but never for an Englishman. He was not an Englishman, and it is hopeless to endeavour to understand him either as man or artist unless that fact is remembered. In *The Foreigner at Home*, written in 1881, Stevenson himself says that "a Scotsman may tramp the better part of Europe and the United States, and never again receive so vivid an impression of foreign travel and strange lands and manners as on his first excursion into England."

The two peoples are spiritually as the poles asunder. "A Scotsman is vain, interested in himself and others, eager for sympathy, setting forth his thoughts and experience in the best light. The egoism of the Englishman is self-contained. He does not seek to proselytise. He takes no interest in Scotland or the Scots, and, what is the unkindest cut of all, he does not care to justify his indifference. Give him the wages of going on and being an Englishman, that is all he asks ; and in the meantime, while you continue to associate, he would rather not be reminded of your baser origin. Compared with the grand, tree-like self-sufficiency of his demeanour, the vanity and curiosity of the Scot seem uneasy, vulgar, and immodest."

This passage seems to suggest that the Scotsman, with his stubborn character and generally superior education, is never quite at home in England, and that overawed by the " tree-like sufficiency " of the English, he is compelled to be over-emphatic and over-assertive. I do not think this is altogether true. As a matter of fact all minorities suffer from a superiority complex. The Jew would never have continued to exist in the modern world, with but not of the people with whom he walks and talks and buys and sells and nowadays even eats, if he were not convinced at the bottom of his soul that, being a Jew, he is the superior of his fellows. The same feeling in a smaller way is shared by all aliens. Without it, the irritations incidental to life in a foreign land would be intolerable. The Scotsman in England is, as I contend, essentially an alien in a foreign land, and he is naturally insistent on his moral and intellectual superiority.

Moreover, Scotland was, and perhaps still is, a poorer country than England, and it is necessary for the poor man's self-respect to make the rich thoroughly realise that he is the better man. The patriotism of a citizen of a small and poor country is something far finer than the patriotism of a citizen of a great and mighty empire. Johnson said that " a Scotsman must be a sturdy moralist who does not prefer Scotland to truth." That was a considerable compliment, though it probably was not intended.

It was true of Stevenson that, to quote Johnson's gibe, " the noblest prospect that the Scotsman ever sees is the high road that leads him to London." He was always ill in his native land. He generally left it with a sigh of relief. He wrote of Edinburgh : " For all who love shelter and the blessing of the sun, who hate dark weather and perpetual tilting against squalls, there could scarcely be found a more unhomely and harassing place of residence." But, until the later years of his life, whenever he was away from Scotland, there was always the yearn for the return home at the back of his mind. And however cosmopolitan he liked to think himself—the average Scotsman is far more cosmopolitan than the average Englishman—he remained a Scotsman in his bone and his marrow until the last days in the South Seas. He said himself : " Even though a Scotsman may acquire the southern knack of talking, he will still have a strong Scots accent of the mind."

To take his own definition of a Scotsman, Stevenson was certainly vain, certainly immensely interested in himself, certainly hungry for affection and sympathy, certainly always concerned to set himself in the best light. But in all this he resembled many other men born south of the Tweed. He ignored the essentials of himself.

The great outstanding characteristic of Scotland is that it is a religious country. Its national life, intellectual as well as spiritual, is built on the Shorter Catechism which, by the way, was written in Westminster. Henley was amazed and indignant to discover that " the Stevenson who never came back from America " was a Shorter Catechist. The truth is, that because he was a Scot, Stevenson was always a Shorter Catechist. " I do not wish," he wrote, " to make an idol of the Shorter Catechism." He endeavoured to escape from it. He never succeeded. No Scotsman, indeed, unless he be born outside the Presbyterian faith, ever escapes. Mr. Chesterton says that Stevenson was far more a Casuist than a Catechist. But he was a Casuist because he was a Catechist.

The Scottish character remains the one great creation of the Reformation. Writing of his father in his *Memories and Portraits*, Stevenson refers to his " blended sternness and softness that was wholly Scottish." A few pages farther on he speaks of Celtic traits. But there is little that is Celtic in modern Edinburgh, as little indeed as there is in modern Dublin. The Scottish character derives from Geneva far more than from the Celtic twilight. In Scotland and perhaps nowhere else, the Reformation was a popular movement, a successful revolt against feudalism in State as well as in Church, an emancipation from thraldom, the birth of a nation. In *The Influence of the Reformation on the Scottish Character*, Froude says :

" In Scotland, the commons, as an organized body, were simply created by religion. Before the Reformation they had no political existence ; and therefore it has been that the print of their origin has gone so deeply into their social constitution. On them, and them only, the burden of the work of the Reformation was eventually thrown ; and when they triumphed at last, it was inevitable that both they and it should react one upon the other.

" Long-headed, thrifty industry, a sound hatred of all waste, imprudence, idleness, extravagance, —the feet planted firmly upon the earth,—a conscientious sense that the worldly virtues are, nevertheless, very necessary virtues, that without these, honesty for one thing is not possible, and that without honesty no other excellence, religious or moral, is worth anything at all,—this is the stuff of which Scotch life was made, and very good stuff it is." [1]

[1] *The Influence of the Reformation on the Scottish Character*, in *Odds and Ends*.

John Knox has been without question the most influential and the most formidable of Scottish worthies, and as Mr. Edwin Muir has recently written, " It was the Church Triumphant in Geneva that finally turned him into the marvellous instrument that changed the fate of Scotland, the fate and the character too." [1]   There is abundant justification for Mr. Muir's assertions that Calvinism " lopped off from religion music, painting, and sculpture, and pruned architecture to a minimum ; it frowned on all prose and poetry which was not sacred," and for the statement " what Knox really did was to rob Scotland of all the benefits of the Renaissance." [2]   But artist though he was, Stevenson had a sneaking admiration both for Calvinism and for John Knox. To Stevenson Knox's character was " strong, salient, and worthy," and he envied the reformer, " with his godly females all leaving their husbands to follow after him."   Whether Knox is regarded with admiration or with a certain aversion, one thing is unquestionable, and that is that, thanks to him and to Calvinism, the Scottish became, and largely remain, an essentially religious nation.

Since the Reformation the majority of Englishmen have been indifferent to religion.   There have been notable religious revivals in England— the Methodist revival, the Evangelical revival in the Church of England that followed it, the Trac-

[1] *John Knox*, by Edwin Muir, p. 308.   [2] *Ibid.*, p. 309.

tarian movement that has brought back a large
measure of sweetness and light to the English
Church, and has vastly added to its bishops' per-
plexities. But for nearly four hundred years, religion has been, for England generally, something
to be formally regarded, say by attendance at
top-hat Mattins, but never to be discussed, or else
something to be entirely neglected. Puritanism
had an effect on the character of the English
middle class, but by the nineteenth century English Puritanism had become Podsnappery. Puritanism never had much effect in England on the
governing class, that maintained its influence into
this century, or on the mass of the people. But,
while for the majority south of the border, religion has been, at the best, a mere respectable
adjunct of life, north of the border it has been for
the majority the very basis of life. Even now no
Scotsman can possibly remain just indifferent to
Calvinism and John Knox. With Carlyle he
must ascribe to them all that is finest in the
national character, or with David Hume he must
hold them responsible for deplorable hypocrisy
and fanaticism, or with Burns he must hate them
and revolt against them.

Stevenson was brought up in a religious atmosphere. His mother was a daughter of the manse.
His father, Sir Graham Balfour says, " clung with
a desperate intensity to the rigid tenets of his
faith." His nurse was a woman of extreme piety,

who taught her charge to pray that his father and mother might not be eternally damned for playing whist. He was suckled on the Shorter Catechism. As he himself said, his was a " Covenanting childhood."

No man ever really escapes from the influence of his early environment. The Roman Catholics recognise this, and insist that their children shall be educated in Roman Catholic schools. The Bolshevists realise that, if Russia is to remain a Communist republic, Bolshevism must be inculcated in the schools, and the Fascists know that, if their grandiose dreams for Italy are to become fact, school children must be taught an aggressive patriotism. It is true that there is often a sharp reaction against a pious upbringing. The clergyman's daughter may often go to the devil, but she always knows that she is going to the devil, while other erring daughters have no idea that the devil exists.

In the religion of Scotland there are particular elements that ensure the permanence of its influence. What man who, in his boyhood, has been present at the solemn Saturday evening preparation for Sacrament Sunday, who has listened to the earnest family prayers, who has intimate experience of the kindness that can accompany earnestness and inflexibility of faith, can ever forget or can ever entirely escape ?

It may be suggested that Stevenson the artist

and dreamer must of necessity have rebelled against the dour family creed and practice, and the youthful escapades in Edinburgh, of which far too much has been written, may seem to confirm this suggestion.   Sir Sidney Colvin, indeed, has written :

" The ferment of youth was more acute and more prolonged in him than in most men even of genius.   There met in him many various strains and elements, which were in these days pulling one against another in his half-formed being at a great expense of spirit and body.   Add the storms, which from time to time attacked him, of shivering repulsion for the climate and conditions of life in the city which he yet deeply and imaginatively loved ;   the moods of spiritual revolt against the harsh doctrines of the creed in which he had been brought up, and to which his parents were deeply, his father even passionately, attached ;   the seasons of temptation, most strongly besetting the ardent and poetic temperament, to seek solace among the crude allurements of the city streets." [1]

Stevenson was certainly unhappy in his adolescence.   He had begun to doubt his father's faith. He was bored by the rigidity of his father's rule of conduct.   Sex burned fiercely in him.   He was weary of Edinburgh.   He was determined to be neither lawyer nor engineer.   " Edinburgh," he

[1] *R. L. S. Letters*, vol. i., Introd., p. 8.

wrote in 1878, " pays cruelly for her high seat in one of the vilest climates under heaven." But if he strayed from the narrow path, he knew quite well that he was straying.

Mr. Chesterton says of Charles II. that "there was something Scotch about his combination of doing what he liked with knowing what he was doing." Stevenson certainly knew what he was doing He knew, for instance, that he was sorely grieving his father and mother. " What a curse I am to my parents ! " he wrote during the Edinburgh student days. " O Lord, what a pleasant thing it is to have just damned the happiness of (prob-ably) the only two people who care a damn about you in the world." Here there are exaggera-tion and sincerity. The two things perhaps rarely exist together. But they always did in Stevenson. He was perhaps recalling his student naughtiness when he wrote in *Dr. Jekyll and Mr. Hyde* : " I was no more myself when I laid aside restraint and plunged in shame than when I laboured in the eye of day at the furtherance of knowledge or the relief of sorrow and suffering." A distin-guished Scottish divine still living, who was a con-temporary of Stevenson in his Edinburgh days, has explained why he knew little of him from the fact that while he was trying to keep the Ten Commandments, Stevenson was always trying to break them. He did not succeed very thoroughly. His " plunging into shame " was no great matter.

He may have philandered with the devil, but there was never any serious intrigue, and this he admitted in his essay *Crabbed Age and Youth* : " Those who go to the devil in youth with anything like a fair chance were probably little worth saving from the first." His sins were local. As he said of the night club that John Nicholson frequented : " If it was a sin to go there, then sin was merely local and municipal." Stevenson always had a conscience, the uncomfortable Puritan conscience. That was part of his heritage. He wrote in one of his Scottish poems :

> Of a' the ills that flesh can fear,
> The loss o' frien's, the lack o' gear,
> A yowlin' tyke, a glandered mear,
> A lassie's nonsense—
> There 's just ae thing I canna bear,
> An' that 's my conscience.

To Stevenson, too, life, with its incidental cakes and ale, was a very serious business. There is the true Covenanter spirit in his rather sententious— " In his own life, then, a man is not to expect happiness, only to profit by it gladly when it shall arise ; he is on duty here ; he knows not how or why, and does not need to know ; he knows not for what hire, and must not ask." The worst, indeed, that can be said of Stevenson's student days is that he was sometimes the Covenanter on the loose. He rejected a great deal of the Covenanter's belief. But all through his life he was

fundamentally religious after the Covenanter
manner.   In the introduction to his *Lay Morals*
he is scornful of " the conscientious atheist, that
strange and wooden rabbi, and never so strange
and so wooden as when very young."   And I find
a striking revelation of the continuance of the
influence of the Covenanter's childhood in a letter
written to J. A. Symonds in 1885 : " My own
conscience is badly seared ; a want of piety ; yet
I pray for it tacitly every day, believing it, after
courage, the only gift worth having, and its want,
in a man of any claims to honour, quite unpardon-
able."   In this letter, he is the Shorter Catechist
at his best, with no suggestion of the self-approval
and self-righteousness which aroused Henley's
rage.   " When a faith has been trodden out," he
wrote, " we may look for a mean and narrow
population ! "

There are faiths and faiths, but I can find little
justification for Mr. Chesterton's description of
Stevenson as " a highly honourable, responsible,
and chivalrous Pagan."   I contend that he remained to the end a highly honourable, responsible, and chivalrous Scottish Puritan, who is a
very different person to the extremely unchival-
rous English Puritans, who have on occasion
moved Mr. Chesterton to wrath.   And I suggest that Mr. Chesterton admires Stevenson so
sincerely and dislikes Puritanism so thoroughly
that, as he cannot pretend that his hero was a

Catholic, he is bound to insist that he must have been a Pagan. " When Stevenson stepped into the wider world of the Continent with its more graceful logic and even its more graceful vice," says Mr. Chesterton, " he went as one emptied of all the ethics and all the metaphysics of his home." That is just what he did not do. He took the ethics and a good deal of the metaphysics with him, both to the Continent and to the South Seas. Mr. Chesterton himself notes " the vague Scottish tradition of a God of mere power and terror " in Stevenson's latest writing, and it is surely the influence of Scottish ethics that caused him, as Mr. Chesterton notes, grossly to misrepresent Villon in the essay described by Charles Whibley as " a sad aberration in criticism." Certainly Stevenson never escaped, nor did he wish to escape from God. No Hound of Heaven had to make him his quarry. But his God was the Scottish Covenanter's God—I am again indebted to Mr. Chesterton—" the Lord," not " Our Lord " of the Catholic.

Stevenson was always a moralist with the itch to preach. He sometimes realised, however, that it is far better to practise than to preach. When he was twenty-three, he wrote to Mrs. Sitwell: " I am desirous to practise now, rather than to preach, for I know that I should preach badly, and men can more easily forgive faulty practice than dull sermons." The artist and the moralist

were never in conflict in Stevenson. Sir Sidney
Colvin says : " All his life the artist and the
moralist in him alike were in rebellion against the
bourgeois spirit—against timid, negative, and
shuffling substitutes for active and courageous
well-doing—and declined to worship at the shrine
of what he called the bestial goddesses Comfort
and Respectability." Stevenson himself says :
" The soul asks honour and not fame ; to be up-
right, not to be successful ; to be good, not prosperous ; to be essentially, not outwardly, respectable. Does your soul ask profit ? Does it ask
money ? Does it ask the approval of the indifferent herd ? I believe not."

To Stevenson respectability was what the Covenanters used to call " rank conformity, the dead-
liest gag and wet blanket that can be laid on
men." The artist Stevenson was a Scottish Covenanter in a black shirt. When he went out to
startle the *bourgeoisie*, he had embarked on a
religious crusade.

The Scottish Covenanter in the black shirt
lived his life in the shadow of death. " I belong
to that besotted class of man the invalid," he
wrote to Henry James in 1884. " He was never
well, all the years I knew him ; and we looked
upon his life as hanging by the frailest thread,"
wrote Sir Edmund Gosse.[1] " Through all his
varied experiences, his bed was a boat and his

[1] *Critical Kit-Kats*, by Edmund Gosse, p. 280.

boat was a bed," says Mr. Chesterton, and he
adds : " Nobody knew better than he did that
nothing is more terrible than a bed, because it is
always waiting to be a death-bed." I do not
believe that his bed was really terrible to Stevenson, I believe that he vastly enjoyed his adventures in his bed-boat. I believe it was because
" any week he might die " that he was " so bright
and keen and witty." He had no time to waste.
He knew that his days must be few, and he resolved that they should be full.

Stevenson wrote of his father : " Morbid, too,
was his sense of the fleetingness of life and his
concern for death." Thomas Stevenson was the
normal healthy man, who lived his full length of
days. It is unwholesome and morbid for the
healthy always to anticipate a premature end, but
this is a vastly different thing to the contemplation
of death inevitable to a man who is constantly ill.
Sir Sidney Colvin says that *Ordered South* is " the
only one of his writings in which he took the invalid point of view and allowed his health troubles
in any degree to colour his work." Perhaps it is
only in *Ordered South* that there is any suggestion
of the point of view of the sick man who is not
artist, adventurer, and Covenanter in one, but
as a matter of fact Stevenson's health troubles
coloured all his work. " The sick room was the
merest external accident in his life," wrote William
Archer. On the contrary, it was one of the things

that made him the man that he was. Death was always on his doorstep, and he looked out of his window unafraid. In his novels death is a constant heroic adventure. Even Israel Hands in *Treasure Island,* as Professor Raleigh has noted, dies heroically.

Familiarity with death, indeed, filled Stevenson with impatient scorn of those who feared it. "Death is a great and gentle solvent; it has never had justice done to it, no, not by Whitman," he wrote to J. A. Symonds. "As for those crockery chimney-piece ornaments, the *bourgeois* (*quorum pars*), and their cowardly dislike of dying and killing, it is merely one symptom of a thousand how utterly they have got out of touch of life." The normal man rarely thinks of his own death, though it is perhaps true that, without such occasional thought, it is impossible to live either intelligently or well. Stevenson was neither physically nor mentally normal. If he did not, with St. Paul, die daily, he must have acutely realised on waking every morning that it was possible, and even probable, that he would die before the sunset.

It has been said that no prayer is ever repeated with greater sincerity than the third petition of the *Agnus Dei*—"O Lamb of God, that taketh away the sins of the world, grant us Thy peace!"—and it was peace and rest that death offered the man constantly harassed by pain. He wrote to Sir Edmund Gosse from Bournemouth in 1886 :

"The soul of piety was killed long ago by that idea of reward. Nor is happiness, whether eternal or temporal, the reward that mankind seeks. Happinesses are but his wayside campings ; his soul is in the journey ; he was born for the struggle, and only tastes his life in effort and on the condition that he is opposed. How, then, is such a creature, so fiery, so pugnacious, so made up of discontent and aspiration, and such noble and uneasy passions—how can he be rewarded but by rest ? "

He knew that he had to suffer, and he suffered with the fortitude and understanding of his race. He wrote to Henley in 1879 :

"So I learn day by day the value and high doctrinality of suffering. Let me suffer always ; not more than I am able to bear, for that makes a man mad, as hunger drives the wolf to sally from the forest ; but still to suffer some, and never to sink up to my eyes in comfort and grow dead in virtues and respectability. I am a bad man by nature, I suppose ; but I cannot be good without suffering a little."

He was determined that death should be " an awfully fine adventure." " Even if death catch people, like an open pitfall, and in mid-career, laying out vast projects, and planning monstrous foundations, flushed with hope, and their mouths full of boastful language, they should be at once tripped up and silenced : is there not something brave and spirited in such a termination ? And does not life go down with a better grace, foaming in full body over a precipice, than miserably straggling to an end in sandy deltas ? When the Greeks made their fine saying that those whom the gods love die young, I cannot help believing they had this sort of death also in their eye. For surely, at whatever age it overtake the man, this is to die young."

While he waited for death, he refused to be daunted and he refused to be dragooned. Life was hot in his mouth. He had no taste for imitation and no time. The sick man in a hurry is to be seen in the experiments, always distinguished and interesting, with every form of literary expression. There is the gay-souled sick man, more concerned than the healthy man need be to save himself from becoming conventionalised, in the black shirt, the brigand's cloak, and the other pleasant eccentricities of Stevenson's dress. " I shall not wear gloves unless my hands are cold or unless I am born with a delight in them. Dress is my own affair, and that of one other in the world ; that, in fact, and for an obvious reason of any woman who shall chance to be in love with me."

There is a natural revolt against the restrictions surrounding the invalid in a score of recorded childish pranks. Mrs. Stevenson relates a typical example. While they were living at Hyères, " an editor of a notorious London journal, who published scandalous stories concerning private individuals, was prosecuted for libel, found guilty, and punished by imprisonment." Stevenson was delighted, and decided that the happy event must be properly celebrated. " In the evening we placed a candle in each window to serve as an illumination, and lighted a bonfire we had previously prepared in the afternoon for the purpose. My husband, our maid, and I clasped hands and danced round the fire, shouting and laughing." The result was, the next day Stevenson " lay in the pangs of a new malady—sciatica—and on the following evening he had a terrible hemorrhage."

There is the sick man, too, who knows his time is short, in the constant itch to move. He wandered in search of health without, I think, any great hope of finding it, and it was characteristic of him that, as Mr. Chesterton says, " as soon as he came to any place he lost no time in finding a new and better reason for having come there." There was always the one better reason. " I travel," he said, " not to go anywhere but to go."

> I love to be warm by the red fireside,
> I love to be wet with rain ;
> I love to be welcome at lamplit doors,
> And leave the doors again.

To go and to return—and then once more to

go ! It was not until he settled at Vailima that he could say with satisfaction, *j'y suis, j'y reste.* He even tired of Hyères, and he was bored by Bournemouth from the first.

, Finally, there is an intimate connection between Stevenson's race and upbringing and his ill-health and the fact that he was the most conspicuous writer of his day who broke away from the gloomy pessimism of the realists. There were so many reasons why he should have been unhappy. He was determined to be happy. So he left behind him the dank valley of the realist, which is in fact the valley of illusion, and climbed with his readers to the hilltops of romance, where is the dwelling-place of truth. Writing of the realists in his essay, *The Lantern Bearers*, he says that in them " life falls dead like dough, instead of soaring away like a balloon into the colours of the sunset ; each is true ; each inconceivable ; for no man lives in the external truth, among salts and acids, but in the warm, phantasmagoric chamber of his brain, with the painted windows and the storied walls."

Gay of heart and of high courage, Stevenson lived his life and wrote his books with the fine swagger, natural to him, of a D'Artagnan or a Cyrano. The reader will not find in his books the spontaneous gaiety of a Fra Angelico or a Mozart, those laughing cavaliers of the arts, but he will find the reflection of a man born of a tough stock, inspired by a dignified conception of man and the universe inherited from his fathers, who, tried as few men of genius have ever been, has made a contribution of permanent value to literature, and from the details of his life has left behind an inspiring example to his fellows.

Glad did I live and gladly die !

Few men die gladly at forty-four if their lives have been happy. But for the sick man, however thrilling the battle, weariness must come sooner or later in the struggle against the odds.

CHAPTER III

BOYHOOD

" I WAS born," Stevenson says in the *Memoirs of Himself*, " in Edinburgh, in 1850, the 13th of November, my father Thomas Stevenson, my mother Margaret Isabella Balfour. My mother's family, the Balfours of Pilrig, is a good provincial stock ; for near three centuries before my appearance, these Balfours had been judges, advocates, and ministers of the Gospel, and I believe them related to many of the so-called good families of Scotland. My father's family is much more remarkable ; this much at least may be said for it, that its history is unparalleled."

This modest boast, and the family pride that it implies, are characteristically Scottish. Stevenson was immensely interested in his ancestors. He would like to have believed that they had " rallied round Macbeth," but he apparently accepted the family tradition that the Stevensons were of Scandinavian origin, and that "the first of his race came from France as Barber-chirurgeon to Cardinal Beaton." There was little to record of the family until the nineteenth century. " On the whole, the Stevensons may be described as

decent, reputable folk, following honest trades—
millers, maltsters, and doctors, playing the character parts in the Waverley Novels with propriety, if without distinction ; and to an orphan
looking about him in the world for a potential
ancestry, offering a plain and quite unadorned
refuge, equally free from shame and glory."

But with the nineteenth century, " we rose out
of obscurity in a clap." In 1787, Thomas Smith,
a merchant-burgess of Edinburgh, who had
" founded a solid business in lamps and oil,"
married the widowed mother of Robert Stevenson, Robert Louis Stevenson's grandfather, and
in 1799 Robert married his stepfather's daughter,
Jean. As Stevenson admits, " the marriage of a
man of twenty-seven and a girl of twenty who
have lived for twelve years as brother and sister,
is difficult to conceive."

Robert and his stepfather, now also his father-
in-law, were bound together by mutual interests
and the same ambition. The dealer in lamps
and oil had become the engineer of the Board of
Northern Lighthouses, and to this position Robert
succeeded in 1807. His grandson delighted in
the romance of his grandfather's calling. In *Records of a Family of Engineers*, written in Vailima in
1891, he says : " The seas into which his labours
carried the new engineer were still scarce charted,
the coasts still dark ; his way on shore was often
far beyond the convenience of any road ; the

isles in which he must sojourn were still partly
savage. He must toss much in boats ; he must
often adventure on horseback by the dubious
bridle-track through unfrequented wildernesses ;
he must sometimes plant his lighthouse in the very
camp of wreckers ; and he was continually enforced to the vicissitudes of outdoor life. The joy
of my grandfather in this career was strong as the
love of woman. It lasted him through youth and
manhood, it burned strong in age, and at the
approach of death his last yearning was to renew
these loved experiences."

Robert, says Robert Louis, was " a projector of
works in the face of nature, and a modifier of
nature itself." His most notable achievements
were the building of a lighthouse on the Bell Rock,
the Inchcape Rock of Southey's poem, and the
making of a main road into Edinburgh. With all
Stevenson's admiration for his grandfather, the
road did not altogether please his artist soul. He
wrote of it in his essay on *Roads* : " We remember,
as we write, some miles of fine wide highway laid
out with conscious aesthetic artifice through a
broken and richly cultivated tract of country. It
is said that the engineer had Hogarth's line of
beauty in his mind as he laid them down. And
the result is striking. One splendid satisfying
sweep passes with easy transition into another,
and there is nothing to trouble or dislocate the
strong continuousness of the main line of the road.

And yet there is something wanting. There is here no saving imperfection, none of those secondary curves and little trepidations of direction that carry, in natural roads, our curiosity actively along with them. One feels at once that this road has not grown like a natural road, but has been laboriously made to pattern ; and that, while a model may be academically correct in outline, it will always be inanimate and cold." The road might be criticised, but the Bell Rock Lighthouse stood for victory after a protracted struggle. The Eddystone is not submerged even at high tide, but the Bell Rock, eleven miles from land, is "covered at every tide to a depth of twelve feet or more, and has thirty-two fathoms' depth of water within a mile of its eastern edge." The lighthouse was finished in 1811. Three years later Sir Walter Scott visited the rock, seeking material for *The Pirate*, and found Robert Stevenson "a most gentlemanlike and modest man."

Robert's youngest son, Thomas, the father of Robert Louis, was born in Edinburgh in 1818. He was apprenticed to his father's profession, and, in his turn, became engineer to the Board of Northern Lights. His son wrote with proper pride of his family's record : " My father and Uncle David made the third generation, one Smith and two Stevensons, of direct descendants who had been engineers to the Board of Northern Lights ; there is scarce a deep-sea light from the

Isle of Man north about to Berwick, but one of
my blood designed it ; and I have often thought
that to find a family to compare with ours in the
promise of immortal memory, we must go back to
the Egyptian Pharaohs : upon so many reefs and
forelands that not very elegant name of Stevenson is engraved with a pen of iron upon granite.
My name is as well known as that of the Duke of
Argyle among the fishers, the skippers, the seamen, and the masons of my native land.   Whenever I smell salt water, I know I am not far from
one of the works of my ancestors.   The Bell Rock
stands monument for my grandfather ; the Skerry
Vohr for my Uncle Alan ; and when the lights
come out at sundown along the shores of Scotland, I am proud to think they burn more brightly
for the genius of my father."

The family genius for lighthouse building and
engineering consisted, says Sir Graham Balfour,
" chiefly of a sort of instinct for dealing with the
forces of nature and seldom manifested clearly
till called for in actual practice."

The lighthouse builders were men of fervent
piety.   The first of them, the dealer in lamps and
oil, was a member of the Church of Scotland
with, as Miss Rosaline Masson rather quaintly
puts it, " an interval of conscientious membership
of the Baptist Church." [1]   And Stevenson says of
his great-grandfather and his grandfather : " Re-

---

[1] *Life of Robert Louis Stevenson*, by Rosaline Masson, p. 5.

ligious they both were ; conscious, like all Scots, of the fragility and unreality of that scene in which we play our uncomprehended parts ; like all Scots, realising daily and hourly the sense of another will than ours and a perpetual direction in the affairs of life. But the current of their endeavours flowed in a more obvious channel. They had got on so far ; to get on further was their next ambition—to gather wealth, to rise in society, to leave their descendants higher than themselves, to be (in some sense) among the founders of families."

I have already referred to Thomas Stevenson's Puritanism. He was, his son says, " shrewd and childish ; passionately attached, passionately prejudiced ; a man of many extremes, many faults of temper ; and no very stable foothold for himself among life's troubles." The last statement seems, by the way, a sufficiently damning criticism of the Calvinistic faith. Thomas was a professional man, with an international reputation and comparatively ample means. He was no mathematician, but " natural shrewdness, a sentiment of optical laws, and a great intensity of consideration led him to just conclusions." He was a man of considerable general culture and a high Tory.

In 1848, Thomas Stevenson married Margaret Isabella Balfour, the youngest daughter of the Rev. Lewis Balfour, minister of the village of

Colinton in the Pentland Hills. Stevenson wrote much of his father and much of his nurse, but not a line of his mother. Few professional writers, indeed, have ever found it easy to write of their mothers. When she married, Mrs. Stevenson was a beautiful girl of nineteen. She was, Sir Graham Balfour says, a woman of a bright and vivacious disposition, often in ill-health, but with a large measure of her son's courage. " Her undaunted spirit," writes Sir Graham Balfour, " led her, when nearly sixty, to accompany her son, first to America, and then, in a racing schooner, through the remotest groups of the Pacific, finally to settle with him in the disturbed spot where he had chosen his home." [1] In his love of adventure Stevenson was his mother's son.

" I was," wrote Stevenson, " an only child, and it may be in consequence, both intelligent and sickly." There is certainly no evidence that only children are generally either intelligent or sickly, but Stevenson loved to derive back all his qualities and deficiencies to his family. He linked his gifts of imagination and his love of romance with the lighthouses of his ancestors. His intelligence and his constant illness were, he believed, due to the fact that his father had only one child while his grandfather had thirteen, most of whom, by the way, died in infancy ! Who can decide what any of us owe to our immediate forebears ? The

[1] *Life of R. L. Stevenson*, by Graham Balfour, pp. 25, 62 (vol. i.).

two most famous living English painters are the
sons of solicitors. Of the more distinguished con-
temporary English writers, one is the son of a successful house agent, and another the son of a not
very successful professional cricketer. The wind
of genius bloweth where it listeth !

Stevenson's ill-health may have been to some
extent inherited from his mother. The lighthouse builders seem to have been a hardy stock.
But it was certainly due in a large measure to the
damp, unhealthy Edinburgh house in which part
of his childhood was spent. The effect of damp-
ness on genius might be the subject of a suggestive
essay. Stevenson owed his ill-health, which was
to be an essential influence in his life and work,
to a damp house in Edinburgh, and John Donne
was vastly affected by his tenancy of a damp
house in Mitcham.

Stevenson was born three months after the
death of his grandfather, Robert, at 8 Howard
Place, a small two-storeyed house, with an under-
ground basement. When he was two years old,
the family moved to No. 1 Inverleith Terrace, a
house from which Professor Aytoun, the author of
Lays of the Cavaliers, had moved, because of its
discomfort. Robert Louis had been a healthy
baby before the move. The arrival in Inverleith
Terrace was immediately followed by a severe
attack of croup, and the boy remained sickly for
the rest of his life.

Six months earlier, Alison Cunningham, the
" Cummy " to whom, thirty years afterwards, he
dedicated *A Child's Garden of Verse*, was engaged as
the boy's nurse.   Never was nurse more devoted
or charge more loyal and grateful.   Stevenson
wrote : " I have three powerful impressions of
my childhood ; my sufferings when I was sick,
my delights in convalescence at my grandfather's
manse of Colinton, near Edinburgh, and the unnatural activity of my mind after I was in bed
at night."   The remembrance of suffering was
always associated with Cummy's loving care :
   " My recollection of the long nights when I was
kept awake by coughing are only relieved by the
thought of the tenderness of my nurse and second
mother (for my first will not be jealous), Alison
Cunningham.   She was more patient than I can
suppose of an angel ; hours together she would
help console me in my paroxysms ; and I remember with particular distinctness, how she would
lift me out of bed, and take me, rolled in blankets,
to the window, whence I might look forth into the
blue night starred with street lamps, and see
where the gas still burned behind the windows of
other sickrooms."
   But devoted as Cummy was, it is doubtful
if her influence over a weak imaginative child
was very wholesome.   His " high-strung religious
ecstasies and terrors " were the result of his nurse's
teaching, and his mother might well be shocked

when she heard what the child had suffered in consequence :

" I would not only lie awake to weep for Jesus, which I have done many a time, but I would fear to trust myself to slumber lest I was not accepted and should slip, ere I awoke, into eternal ruin. I remember repeatedly, although this was later on, and in the new house, waking from a dream of Hell, clinging to the horizontal bar of the bed, with my knees and chin together, my soul shaken, my body convulsed with agony. It is not a pleasant subject. I piped and snivelled over the Bible, with an earnestness that had been talked into me. I would say nothing without adding, ' if I am spared,' as though to disarm fate by a show of submission ; and some of this feeling still remains upon me in my thirtieth year. I shook my numskull over the spiritual welfare of my parents, because they gave dinner parties and played cards, things contemned in the religious biographies on which my mind was fed."

The manse at Colinton, with the old dignified grandfather, its garden and the gardener, was a pleasant place of escape from the dank Edinburgh house. Stevenson described his grandfather's garden in a paper published in 1887 : " It was a place in that time like no other : the garden cut into provinces by a great hedge of beech, and over-looked by the church and the terrace of the church-yard, where the tombstones were thick, and after

nightfall 'spunkies' might be seen to dance at
least by children ; flower-plots lying warm in sunshine ; laurels and the great yew making elsewhere a pleasing horror of shade ; the smell of
water rising from all round, with an added tang
of paper-mills ; the sound of water everywhere,
and the sound of mills—the wheel and the dam
singing their alternate strain ; the birds on every
bush and from every corner of the overhanging
woods pealing out their notes until the air
throbbed with them ; and in the midst of this,
the manse."

His mother's father was, Stevenson said, " the
noblest looking old man I have ever seen," strict,
Spartan, unapproachable. " I often wonder,"
wrote Stevenson, ever bothered by the problems
of heredity, " what I have inherited from this old
minister. I must suppose indeed that he was fond
of preaching sermons, and so am I, though I never
heard it maintained that either of us loved to hear
them. . . . He loved port, and nuts, and porter ;
and so do I, but they agreed better with my grandfather, which seems to me a breach of contract."
The angel of the manse was Aunt Jane, who was
nearly blind and deaf, but contrived also to be
" the most serviceable and amiable of women and
the family maid-of-all-work," constantly mother-
ing some or other of her almost innumerable
nephews and nieces.

When he was five, Stevenson first met his

cousin, Robert Alan Stevenson, who was to be
one of his most intimate friends, and when he was
six, he began his career as a writer. An uncle had
offered a prize for the best *History of Moses*, and
Stevenson dictated his version to his mother. It
reflects the piety of the Covenanter's home, and
is remarkable writing for a child of six, even if
it was lovingly sub-edited by his mother. The
following is the moral of the tale : " Then God
told Moses to take some brass and soften it in the
fire and to cut it into the shape of one of the ser-
pents and to put it upon a pole and to hold up the
pole and the Israelites who looked at the serpent
would get better. That should put us in mind of
Jesus, because the old Serpent the Devil bit us,
that means made us naughty and when we look
at Jesus that makes us better—not to look at
Jesus with our eyes but to look with praying."

Sir Graham Balfour prints extracts from Mrs.
Stevenson's diary which suggest that her small
son was rather smug and very precocious. Recalling his baby years when he was a man of
thirty, Stevenson found his pious upbringing
cruel because it brought " a child among the
awful shadows of a man's life," and unwise because " the idea of sin, attached to particular
actions absolutely, far from repelling, soon exerts
an attraction on young minds." Had he died as
a child, he might, he supposes, have " figured in
a tract," and on the whole he had not much joy

in remembering his early years. But Stevenson
was never a hard judge of himself. Henley has
described the Stevenson of Sir Graham's Life as
" this Seraph in chocolate, this barley-sugar effigy
of a man." [1] The description is ridiculous, but it
is impossible not to recall it after reading Stevenson's own picture of his childhood : " In my case
and with all my evil on my head, it is yet true
there was something of the saintly. Not because
I wept over the Saviour's agony ; not because I
could repeat, with some appropriate inflections, a
psalm or two or the story of the Shunamite's son ;
but because I had a great fund of simplicity, believed all things, and the good rather than the
evil, was very prone to love and inaccessible to
hatred, and never failed in gratitude for any
benefit I had the wit to understand. The sight
of deformed persons and above all of hideous old
women moved in me a sort of panic horror ; yet
I can well recall with what natural courtesy I
strove to conceal my disaffection."

Happily for Stevenson and the world, the saint-
liness of the youthful Covenanter was modified by
excursions into what Mr. Chesterton has called
" the Country of Skelt." He and his cousin became the possessors of a cardboard theatre, manu-
factured by the famous Mr. Skelt, the delights of
which, with proper tribute to its maker, he has
recorded in his delightful essay, *A Penny Plain and*

[1] *Pall Mall Magazine*, September to December 1901.

Twopence Coloured. Cummy was probably disturbed by the presence of a toy theatre in the Calvinist nursery, but *The Red Rover, The Wood Daemon, Jack Sheppard, My Poll and my Partner Joe,* and *Three-Fingered Jack, the Terror of Jamaica,* must have been admirable antidotes to the masterpieces of " a whole crowd of dismal and morbid devotees," regularly read to the boy by his nurse.

In February 1857 Stevenson had an attack of bronchitis, and his parents at last resolved to move from their mildewed abode to a large sunny house, No. 17 Heriot Row, where they remained until Thomas Stevenson's death. In the summer of this year Stevenson first went to school, but only for a few weeks. He had gastric fever in the autumn, and there was no more schooling for him until 1859. In 1861 he was sent to the Edinburgh Academy, where he stayed for a year and a half, and then, for one term, he went to an English boarding school at Isleworth. His mother was ill and had to winter abroad, and kindly Aunt Jane had settled in London after the death of her father, the minister of Colinton, in 1860. Stevenson, an odd, delicate, moody boy, who played no games, though he could ride and swim, was unhappy at the Edinburgh Academy and unhappy at Isleworth. " My dear papa," he wrote to his father from Isleworth, " you told me to tell you whenever I was miserable. I do not feel well, and I wish to get home. Do take me with you."

Stevenson wrote of his Scottish and English schoolfellows : " I have been to school in both countries, and I found, in the boys of the North, something at once rougher and more tender, at once more reserve and more expansion, a greater habitual distance chequered by glimpses of a nearer intimacy, and on the whole wider extremes of temperament and sensibility. The boy of the South seems more wholesome, but less thoughtful ; he gives himself to games as to a business, striving to excel, but is not readily transported by imagination ; the type remains with me as cleaner in mind and body, more active, fonder of eating, endowed with a lesser and a less romantic sense of life and of the future, and more immersed in present circumstances. And certainly, for one thing, English boys are younger for their age."

In 1864 he was at a day school in Edinburgh which, Sir Graham Balfour says, he attended " with more or less regularity " until 1867. The intermittent attendance at school was caused by his own ill-health and his mother's. There was compensation for the loss in private tutoring, wide reading, and the beginning of the wandering that was to be the outstanding feature of Stevenson's life. When he was seven, he was taken to the English lakes. When he was twelve, he was taken to the Isle of Wight. In the summer of the same year he was in Homburg, and in January 1863 he paid his first visit to the Riviera, afterwards going on a sort of Sir Henry Lunn's tour through Italy and Germany. It has been noted as a curious fact that Rome and the other Italian cities made no apparent impression on the boy, now, " fair, tall, a rather narrow figure, a very enquiring mind and very fond of discussing all round any question that interested him." [1]   Christmas 1863 was spent on the Riviera, and the two next springs in Torquay. The boy of fifteen had seen many countries, talked to many people, read many books. He had learned to play picquet from a French tutor in Mentone, and he first read Dumas in a hotel in Nice.   In his essay, *Books which have Influenced Me*, which first appeared in the *British Weekly*, then conducted by that shrewd editor, Sir William Robertson Nicoll, he says : " Perhaps my dearest and best friend outside of Shakespeare is D'Artagnan—the elderly D'Artagnan of the *Vicomte de Bragelonne*.   I know not a more human soul, nor, in his way, a finer ; I shall be very sorry for the man who is so much of a pedant in morals that he cannot learn from the Captain of Musketeers.   Lastly, I must name the *Pilgrim's Progress*, a book that breathes of every beautiful and valuable emotion."

In his *Gossip on a Novel of Dumas's* he writes : " My acquaintance with the *Vicomte* began, somewhat indirectly, in the year of grace 1863, when I had the advantage of studying certain illus-

[1] *Life of Robert Louis Stevenson*, by Rosaline Masson, p. 45.

trated dessert plates in a hotel at Nice. The name
of D'Artagnan in the legends I already saluted
like an old friend, for I had met it the year before
in a work of Miss Yonge's. My first perusal was
in one of those pirated editions that swarmed at
that time out of Brussels, and ran to such a troop
of neat and dwarfish volumes.''

He read Scott and Thackeray, and Harrison
Ainsworth and Bunyan and (an odd enough
choice for a boy) George Sand, and Scottish
history in particular. And always he had the
itch to write. Many men destined to be bank
managers and Members of Parliament have had
literary ambition in their boyhood, and it would
be absurd to attach any importance to Stevenson's contributions to school magazines even when
he was their editor. But the essay, *The Pentland
Rising : A Page of History, 1666,* has interest. It
was written when Stevenson was sixteen, and it
shows wide knowledge of the Covenanter writers
and of that prejudiced English Whig, Bishop
Burnet. It also demonstrates that, however dis-
similar in character Stevenson may have been to
his fellows, he was a Covenanter in his bone and
marrow. Stevenson had originally intended that
The Pentland Rising should be a novel, but his
father persuaded him to make it a historical study.
It was published anonymously at his father's
expense in an edition of a hundred copies, at the
price of fourpence a copy.

In the autumn of 1867, Stevenson was entered at Edinburgh University. It was still understood that he was to carry on the family tradition and build lighthouses, and he had already accompanied his father in his visits of inspection to the Northern lights.

These visits had a lasting effect on his mind and character. Actually to inspect the family's achievements intensified the family pride. It accentuated his taste for adventure and his love of the sea. He says in the *Education of an Engineer* : " It takes a man into the open air ; it keeps him hanging about harbour-sides ; which is the richest form of idling ; it carries him to wild islands ; it gives him a taste of the genial dangers of the sea ; it supplies him with dexterities to exercise ; it makes demands upon his ingenuity ; it will go far to cure him of any taste (if ever he had one) for the miserable life of cities. And when it has done so, it carries him back and shuts him in an office ! From the roaring skerry and the wet thwart of the tossing boat, he passes to the stool and desk ; and with a memory full of ships, and seas, and perilous headlands, and the shining pharos, he must apply his long-sighted eyes to the petty niceties of drawing, or measure his inaccurate mind with several pages of consecutive figures. He is a wise youth, to be sure, who can balance one part of genuine life against two parts of drudgery between four walls, and for the sake of the one, manfully accept the other."

Stevenson always loved the open air. Perhaps he was never quite so happy as in the canoe with Walter Simpson, or in the Cevennes with Modestine, resting " in God's green caravanserai." He says in *Travels with a Donkey* : " To wash in one of God's rivers in the open air seems to me a sort of cheerful solemnity or semi-pagan act of worship. To dabble among dishes in a bedroom may perhaps make clean the body ; but the imagination takes no share in the cleansing."

He was always, too, a specialist in idling. " There is nothing better in life," he said, " than to lounge before the inn door in the sunset, or lean over the parapet of the bridge, to watch the weeds and the quick fishes." He hung about harbours in his youth. He hung about South Sea beaches in after years collecting material for romances from gossip with beachcombers. He found a wild enough island in Earraid, off Mull, where David Balfour was shipwrecked in *Kidnapped*, " a jumble of granite rocks and heather in among." He was to find strange islands before his death. And he never tired of " the genial dangers of the seas."

CHAPTER IV

THE COVENANTER IN REVOLT

STEVENSON was nominally a student at Edinburgh University from 1867 to 1873. " The truth is," according to a fellow-student whom Miss Masson quotes, " that Stevenson never was a University student in the usual sense of the word, not only was his attendance at classes intermittent, but he followed no regular curriculum. Then he took very little part in the work of the classes which he did attend." [1] His fellow-students knew that he was an only child and need never want. " They had their living to earn and could not afford to waste time with apparent idlers." [1] Stevenson himself admits to the " infinite yawnings during lectures and unquenchable gusto in the delights of truantry " experienced by " a certain lean, ugly, idle, unpopular student." Sir Graham Balfour says that " No one ever played the truant with more deliberate care." But he was industrious in his own way. He says : " All through my boyhood and youth, I was known and pointed out for the pattern of an idler ; and yet I was always busy on my own private end, which

[1] *Life of Robert Louis Stevenson,* by Rosaline Masson, pp. 60, 61.

was to learn to write. I kept always two books in
my pocket, one to read, one to write in. As I
walked, my mind was busy fitting what I saw
with appropriate words ; when I sat by the road-
side, I would either read, or a pencil and a penny
version-book would be in my hand, to note down
the features of the scene or commemorate some
halting stanzas. Thus I lived with words. . . .
Whenever I read a book or a passage that particularly pleased me, in which a thing was said or
an effect rendered with propriety, in which there
was either some conspicuous force or some happy
distinction in the style, I must sit down at once
and set myself to ape that quality. I was unsuccessful, and I knew it ; and tried again, and
was again unsuccessful and always unsuccessful ;
but at least in these vain bouts, I got some practice in rhythm, in harmony, in construction and
the co-ordination of parts. I have thus played
the sedulous ape to Hazlitt, to Lamb, to Words-
worth, to Sir Thomas Browne, to Defoe, to Haw-
thorne, to Montaigne, to Baudelaire, and to
Obermann."

The youth living " with words " and dreaming
of literary fame had no serious intention of spending his life building lighthouses, nor do I believe
that, as Mrs. Stevenson has written, he really
wanted to be a soldier. He was born for the
weaving of words.

The idle student was shunned by the indus-

D

trious. He was eccentric in conduct and dress. He was curious and adventurous, and it was inevitable that he should find companions in the stews—seamen, chimney-sweeps, and thieves. According to his own account quoted by Sir Graham Balfour, his " circle was being continually changed by the action of the police magistrate." He was known to his friends as Velvet Coat. They were all very kind and gentle to him as he sat among them " generally in silence and making sonnets in a penny version-book." [1] Indeed, he cannot have been a very lucrative companion, since his father only allowed him twelve pounds a year pocket-money.

To the staid citizen the picture of a boy in a velvet coat sitting among harlots and thieves, writing sonnets in a penny exercise-book, is ridiculous. But Stevenson recalled it with a queer pride and, as proof of his popularity, he recorded that the proprietor of the particular haunt that he frequented sometimes invited him to tea with his mistress ! It is not to be supposed that it was either to write sonnets in a congenial atmosphere or to have tea with a brothel keeper that really induced Stevenson to spend his time with outcasts. He felt something of an outcast himself. He enjoyed feeling himself an outcast, and he always had a genuine sympathy with the despised and rejected, whatever might be their sins.

[1] *Life of R. L. Stevenson*, by Graham Balfour, p. 84 (vol. i.).

In this connection, there is a striking entry in his Note Book :

" The harm of prostitution lies not in itself, but in the disastrous moral influence of ostracism. This *decivilisation*, this rejection of individuals or classes from the social commonwealth, would have its own natural result, whosoever was the individual or the class upon which it was brought to bear. Hunted religionists become cruel and inhuman, just as ostracised harlots do ; only the different other conditions produce cruelty and inhumanity in different shapes. It must be remembered, however, that prostitution is quite beyond parallel in this particular circumstance, that the pariah is obliged to homologate the justice of the *capitis diminutio* to which she is condemned. A Jew, a Christian, a Mormon, or a Thug were proud of the reproach, and wear the byeword as a distinction ; while you may make a prostitute cry by merely naming her trade to her. If you think seriously of all the depressing, demoralising, decivilising influences brought to bear upon her, I think you will find it matter for wonder not that she is so fallen, but that she is still (and that in so many instances) as honest, kind, and decent as she is."

There is nothing very unusual in these youthful adventures, nothing very significant, certainly nothing in the least heroic. The Covenanter was on the loose—but not for very long. " I do not believe," he said, " these days were among the least happy I have spent." He loved pretending. He was something of a *poseur* as he was always a *charmeur*. He was, as Henley called him, " the good and constant histrion."

It cannot be denied that Thomas Stevenson was, to some extent, responsible for his son's irresponsibility. The boy had never been disciplined at school. His ill-health had covered a multitude of irregularities, and it is odd that so shrewd a man as his father should have supposed that the result of a haphazard upbringing could possibly be a successful engineer. Fortunately for him his pocket-money was limited.

But everything was done for his comfort. He had his own rooms in the house in Heriot Row, and, in 1867, with his son's health in mind, his father leased a house at Swanston at the foot of the Pentland Hills. Swanston, Miss Masson says, gripped Stevenson's heart from the beginning, and he remembered it so well that twenty years after he used it as a scene in *St. Ives*, the novel that he left unfinished. He came to know and to love the country folk, and the Swanston days have their memorial in the description of the old Scottish gardener which appeared in the Edinburgh *University Magazine* in 1871 :

" He was a man whose very presence could impart a savour of quaint antiquity to the baldest and most modern flower-plots. There was a

dignity about his tall stooping form, and an
earnestness in his wrinkled face that recalled Don
Quixote ; but a Don Quixote who had come
through the training of the Covenant, and been
nourished in his youth on *Walker's Lives* and *The
Hind Let Loose.*"

As a matter of fact little of his Edinburgh time
was actually spent with "seamen and chimney-
sweeps." He was a member of the University
Conservative Club and was elected to the Specu-
lative Society, a university society of considerable
repute, which was limited to thirty ordinary
members. Stevenson addressed the society on
the abolition of capital punishment and on the
influence of the Covenanting persecutions on the
Scottish mind, and this interest in serious things
must have been some compensation to his father,
when his son was hailed before the magistrates
for taking part in a town and gown fight.

Thomas Stevenson was often bewildered by his
son, and sometimes bitterly disappointed, but it
is grossly unfair to suggest that he was ever harsh
or niggardly. It took him some time to realise
his son's genius, but when he had realised it, he
had the utmost pride in it, and though in the
student days he wisely limited the money that
could be wasted on " the chimes at midnight," he
fed and clothed his son and entertained his friends,
paid his debts and, in after years, made a literary
career possible by liberal allowances. It must be

remembered, too, that for three and a half years Stevenson allowed his father to suppose that he seriously intended to be an engineer. It is possible, as Sir Sidney Colvin says, that the disagreements with his father seriously affected Stevenson's health. It is certain that in the later days of a fuller understanding, the disagreements were often remembered and regretted. There is a scene in the *Misadventures of John Nicholson*, in which old Nicholson, righteously angry with his son, declares : " I rose this morning what the world calls a happy man—happy, at least, in a son of whom I thought I could be reasonably proud." And the son bitterly answers : " How could I tell you were proud of me ? Oh ! I wish, I wish that I had known ! "

The father and son in *The Story of a Lie* are obviously Thomas Stevenson and Robert Louis : " He had a hearty respect for Dick as a lad of parts. Dick had a respect for his father as the best of men, tempered by the politic revolt of a youth who has to see his own independence. Whenever the pair argued, they came to an open rupture ; and arguments were frequent, for they were both positive, and both loved the work of the intelligence." The more painful relations between father and son in *Weir of Hermiston* are also reminiscent of Stevenson's Edinburgh days :

" An idea of Archie's attitude, since we are all grown up and have forgotten the days of our

youth, it is more difficult to convey. He made
no attempt whatsoever to understand the man
with whom he dined and breakfasted. Parsi-
mony of pain, glut of pleasure, these are the two
alternating ends of youth ; and Archie was of the
parsimonious. The wind blew cold out of a certain quarter—he turned his back upon it ; stayed
as little as was possible in his father's presence ;
and when there, averted his eyes as much as was
decent from his father's face. The lamp shone
for many hundred days upon these two at table—
my lord ruddy, gloomy, and unreverent ; Archie
with a potential brightness that was always
dimmed and veiled in that society ; and there
were not, perhaps, in Christendom two men more
radically strangers. The father, with a grand
simplicity, either spoke of what interested himself, or maintained an unaffected silence. The
son turned in his head for some topic that should
be quite safe, that would spare him fresh evidences
either of my lord's inherent grossness or of the
innocence of his inhumanity ; treading gingerly
the ways of intercourse, like a lady gathering up
her skirts in a by-path. If he made a mistake,
and my lord began to abound in matter of offence,
Archie drew himself up, his brow grew dark, his
share of the talk expired ; but my lord would faithfully and cheerfully continue to pour out the worst
of himself before his silent and offended son."

In the summer of 1868 Stevenson went to

Anstruther on the coast of Fife and to Wick to gain practical experience of the work of his father's firm. In the next year he went to the Orkneys and Shetlands, and in 1870 he made a tour of the Western Islands. He loved the sea, but he hated the work and the drabness. " I am utterly sick of this grey grim sea beaten hole," he wrote to his mother from Anstruther. " I have a little cold in my head, which makes my eyes sore ; and you can't tell how utterly sick I am, and how anxious to get back among trees and flowers and something less meaningless than this bleak fertility."

" In Wick," he wrote, " I have never heard any one greet his neighbour with the usual ' Fine day ' or ' Good morning.' Both come shaking their heads, and both say, ' Breezy, breezy ! ' And such is the atrocious quality of the climate, that the remark is almost invariably justified by the fact.

" The streets are full of the Highland fishers, lubberly, stupid, inconceivably lazy and heavy to move. You bruise against them, tumble them over, elbow them against the wall—all to no purpose ; they will not budge ; and you are forced to leave the pavement every step."

At Wick, " one of the meanest of man's towns," Stevenson had his one experience of diving, related in *The Education of an Engineer* :

" Safe in my cushion of air, I was conscious of

no impact ; only swayed idly like a weed, and was now borne helplessly abroad, and now swiftly—and yet with dream-like gentleness—impelled against my guide. So does a child's balloon divagate upon the currents of the air, and touch and slide off again from every obstacle. So must have ineffectually swung, so resented their inefficiency, those light clouds that followed the Star of Hades, and uttered exiguous voices in the land beyond Cocytus.

" There was something strangely exasperating, as well as strangely wearying, in these uncommanded evolutions. It is bitter to return to infancy, to be supported, and directed, and perpetually set upon your feet, by the hand of some-one else. The air besides, as it is supplied to you by the busy millers on the platform, closes the eustachian tubes and keeps the neophyte perpetually swallowing, till his throat is grown so dry that he can swallow no longer. And for all these reasons—although I had a fine, dizzy, muddle-headed joy in my surroundings, and longed, and tried, and always failed, to lay hands on the fish that darted here and there about me, swift as humming-birds—yet I fancy I was rather relieved than otherwise when Bain brought me back to the ladder and signed to me to mount. And there was one more experience before me even then. Of a sudden, my ascending head passed into the trough of a swell. Out of the green, I shot at

once into a glory of rosy, almost of sanguine light
—the multitudinous seas incarnadined, the heaven
above a vault of crimson. And then the glory
faded into the hard, ugly daylight of a Caithness
autumn, with a low sky, a grey sea, and a whist-
ling wind."

During the tour in the Hebrides, in 1870, he
first met Edmund Gosse, who was to be one of his
closest and dearest friends. Sir Edmund has related that at the port of Portree " a company of
importance in their day " came on board his
steamer. " There were also several engineers of
prominence. At the tail of this chatty, jesting
little crowd of invaders came a youth of about
my own age, whose appearance, for some mysterious reason, instantly attracted me. He was tall,
preternaturally lean, with longish hair, and as
restless and questing as a spaniel. The party
from Portree fairly took possession of us ; at
meals they crowded around the captain, and we
common tourists sat silent, below the salt. The
stories of Blackie and Sam Bough were resonant.
Meanwhile, I know not why, I watched the plain,
pale lad who took the lowest place in this privi-
leged company.

" The summer of 1870 remains in the memory
of western Scotland as one of incomparable splendour. Our voyage, especially as evening drew
on, was like an emperor's progress. We stayed
on deck till the latest moment possible, and I

occasionally watched the lean youth, busy and
serviceable, with some of the little tricks with
which we were later on to grow familiar—the
advance with hand on hip, the sidewise bending
of the head to listen. Meanwhile darkness over-
took us, a wonderful halo of moonlight swam up
over Glenelg, the indigo of the peaks of the
Cuchullins faded into the general blue night. I
went below, but was presently aware of some
change of course, and then of an unexpected
stoppage. I tore on deck, and found that we had
left our track among the islands, and had steamed
up a narrow and unvisited fiord of the mainland
—I think Loch Nevis. The sight was curious and
bewildering. We lay in a gorge of blackness,
with only a strip of the blue moonlit sky overhead ;
in the dark a few lanterns jumped about the shore,
carried by agitated but unseen and soundless
persons. As I leaned over the bulwarks, Stevenson was at my side, and he explained to me that
we had come up this loch to take away to Glasgow
a large party of emigrants driven from their
homes in the interest of a deer forest. . . . When
I came on deck next morning, my unnamed
friend was gone. He had put off with the engineers to visit some remote lighthouse of the
Hebrides." [1]

The two men were not to meet again for seven
years.

<hr />

[1] *Critical Kit-Kats*, by Edmund Gosse, pp. 276, 277.

It was reasonable for Thomas Stevenson to regard these trips as evidence of professional zeal, and
the belief was strengthened, when, in March 1871,
his son read a paper to the Royal Scottish Society
of Arts on *A New Form of Intermittent Light for
Lighthouses*, and was warmly praised. A fortnight
later Stevenson told his father that he was determined to abandon engineering for literature.
This was no new resolve. " I was at that time,"
he said, writing of the year 1873, " as I had
always been, firmly decided upon the career of
letters." His father took his disappointment
calmly, but with a reasonable doubt whether
literature alone would assure an income. He insisted that Robert Louis should read law and be
called to the Scottish Bar.

During the next two years Stevenson attended,
again more or less irregularly, the University
lectures on Civil Law, Public Law, and Political
Economy, and spent part of his time in the offices
of a firm of Writers to the Signet, studying con-
veyancing. He passed the preliminary Bar examination in 1872.

The happiest event of his later student years
was the return to Edinburgh of his cousin, Robert
A. M. Stevenson, afterwards the well-known art
critic. " I was done with the sullens for good ;
there was an end of green-sickness for my life as
soon as I had got a friend to laugh with." The
two cousins laughed together, played the fool with

harmless ingenuity together, and talked interminably. Stevenson himself was an inspired talker. Henley says of him : "He shone in debate, and he excelled in talk. But both in talk and debate he was strung to his highest pitch—alert, daring, of an inextinguishable gaiety, quick and resourceful to the nth degree ; and to try a fall with him then was to get badly handled, if not utterly suppressed." [1]

And of his cousin, Stevenson has written : " I know not which is more remarkable ; the insane lucidity of his conclusions, the humorous eloquence of his language, or his power of method, bringing the whole of life into the focus of the subject treated, mixing the conversational salad like a drunken god. He doubles like the serpent, changes and flashes like the shaken kaleidoscope, transmigrates bodily into the views of others, and so, in the twinkling of an eye, and with a heady rapture, turns questions inside out and flings them empty before you on the ground like a triumphant conjuror." [2]

Among Stevenson's other intimates were Charles Baxter, to whom he wrote many of his published letters, Sir Walter Simpson, the son of the inventor of chloroform, his companion on the *Inland Voyage*, James Walter Ferrier, and Professor and Mrs. Jenkin. His friendship with Ferrier

[1] *Life of R. L. Stevenson*, by Graham Balfour, p. 91 (vol. i.).
[2] *Pall Mall Gazette*, September to December 1901.

inspired Stevenson, when his friend died, to a beautiful tribute in the essay *Old Mortality*, published in *Longman's Magazine* in 1884.

" The powers and the ground of friendship is a mystery ; but, looking back, I can discern that, in part, we loved the thing he was, for some shadow of what he was to be." Ferrier had suffered and failed. " I see the indifferent pass before my friend's last resting-place ; pause, with a shrug of pity, marvelling that so rich an argosy had sunk. A pity, now that he is done with suffering, a pity most uncalled for, and an ignorant wonder. Before those who loved him, his memory shines like a reproach ; they honour him for silent lessons ; they cherish his example ; and in what remains before them of their toil, fear to be unworthy of the dead. For this proud man was one of those who prospered in the valley of humiliation."

Fleeming Jenkin was appointed to the Chair of Engineering in Edinburgh University when he was a man of thirty-eight and Stevenson was still playing at being an engineer. His wife met Stevenson in his mother's drawing-room, " a slender, brown, long-haired lad, with great dark eyes, a brilliant smile and a gentle deprecating bend of the head." She called him " this young Heine with a Scottish accent," and a friendship began that had an obvious effect on Stevenson's development. The Professor of Engineering could hardly have approved the idle student, but the man and perhaps particularly his wife were keenly interested in the odd boy. He played private theatricals at their house. His opinions, already converging from Calvinistic orthodoxy, were influenced by Jenkin, who at that time—he apparently changed his mind later in his life— affected "religion without dogma." In the memoir of Jenkin which Stevenson wrote in 1885, he says :

" His piety was, indeed, a thing of chief importance. His views (as they are called) upon religious matters varied much ; and he could never be induced to think them more or less than views. ' All dogma is to me mere form,' he wrote ; ' dogmas are mere blind struggles to express the inexpressible. I cannot conceive that any single proposition whatever in religion is true in the scientific sense ; and yet all the while I think the religious view of the world is the most true view. Try to separate from the mass of their statements that which is common to Socrates, Isaiah, David, St. Bernard, the Jansenists, Luther, Mahomet, Bunyan—yes, and George Eliot ; of course you do not believe that this something could be written down in a set of propositions like Euclid, neither will you deny that there is something common and this something very valuable.' "

" To try and draw my friend at greater length," Stevenson wrote to his widow, " and say what he was to me and his intimates, what a good influence in life and what an example, is a desire that grows upon me. It was strange, as I wrote the note, how his old tests and criticisms haunted me ; and it reminded me afresh with every few words how much I owe him. . . . Dear me, what happiness I owe to both of you ! "

Stevenson's health had been much better since 1867, and there had been no necessity for wintering abroad, but he was ill again in the winter of 1871, and went to Dunblane for a change in the following spring. The joy in living which was his all the time, and despite all adverse circumstances, is expressed in a letter written to Charles Baxter in which he says : " In such weather one has the bird's need to whistle ; and I, who am specially incompetent in this art, must content myself by chattering away to you on this bit of paper. All the way along I was thanking God that he had made me and the birds and everything just as they are and not otherwise, for, although there was no sun, the air was so thrilled with robins and blackbirds that it made the heart tremble with joy, and the leaves are far enough forward on the underwood to give a fine promise for the future. Even myself, as I say, I would not have had changed in one *iota* this forenoon."

In the summer Stevenson went to Belgium and Germany with Sir Walter Simpson. He liked Brussels very much and Frankfort very little.

" What a falling off after the heavenly afternoons in Brussels." But his vanity was mightily tickled, as it always was, when he was taken for a Frenchman. One of the reasons for the German trip was that he should learn the language, but French remained, throughout his life, the only foreign language that he spoke really well. He went often to the theatre, and there is a curious admission of sentimentality in his remark, in a letter to his mother, that while listening to *La Juive*, presumably Halévy's opera, " I was very near the tear point more than once." That the " penny plain twopence coloured " Stevenson was still alive at twenty-two is suggested in the same letter where he writes :

" An opera is far more *real* than real life to me. It seems as if stage illusion, and particularly this hardest to swallow and most conventional illusion of them all—an opera—would never stale upon me. I wish that life was an opera. I should like to *live* in one ; but I don't know in what quarter of the globe I shall find a Society so constituted. Besides, it would soon fall ; imagine asking for three-kreuzer cigars in recitative, or giving the washerwoman the inventory of your dirty clothes in a sustained and *flourish-ous* aria."

Stevenson joined his father and mother in Baden-Baden, and was back in Edinburgh in October. Four months afterwards occurred his second break with his father. Thomas Stevenson had probably realised that Robert Louis's health made it hopeless for him to carry on the lighthouse business, and had easily got over his disappointment at the breaking of a family tradition. It was quite another matter when his son, " in answer to one or two questions as to beliefs," confessed that he could no longer subscribe to the Covenanter's faith. To his father Stevenson was " a careless infidel." He called himself, only half in jest, " a horrible atheist." As a matter of fact he would probably have, in 1873, agreed with the creed of Fleeming Jenkin, and if his father had realised how much of the Covenanter remained in his son, his grief would assuredly have been assuaged.

Writing to Baxter of the scene with his father and mother, Stevenson said : " Here is a good heavy cross with a vengeance, and all rough with rusty nails that tear your fingers, only it is not I that have to carry it alone ; I hold the light end, but the heavy burden falls on these two."

This letter suggests the self-pity of the complete egoist that Henley and Mr. Benson would have it believed that Stevenson was. But there is, too, an obviously genuine regret that he was compelled to hurt the people whom he loved. It is possible that, as was his habit, Stevenson took the whole thing far too tragically. Certainly in the months that followed, his letters constantly suggest that kindly family relations continued. " I have been to-day a very long walk with my father." " My mother and I wandered about for two hours. We lunched together and were very merry." " My father and I went off for a long walk." " My father and I walked into Dumfries to church." And so on. How deeply Thomas Stevenson felt, however, is shown in Stevenson's account of an interview between his father and his cousin :

" The object of the interview is not very easy to make out ; it had no practical issue except the ludicrous one that Bob promised never to talk Religion to me any more. It was awfully rough on him, you know ; he had no idea that there was that sort of thing in the world, although I had told him often enough—my father on his knees and that kind of thing. . . . I have seen Bob again, and he has had a private letter from my father, apologizing for anything he may have said, but adhering to the substance of the interview. If I had not a very light heart and a great faculty of interest in what is under hand, I really think I should go mad under this wretched state of matters. Even the calm of our daily life is all glossing, there is a sort of tremor through it all and a whole world of repressed bitterness." A fortnight later he wrote : " I have just had another disagreeable to-night. It is difficult indeed to steer steady among the breakers : I am always touching ground ; generally it is my own blame, for I cannot help getting friendly with my father (whom I *do* love), and so speaking foolishly with my mouth. I have yet to learn in ordinary conversation that reserve and silence that I must try to unlearn in the matter of the feelings."

Stevenson seems to have gone out of his way to ask for trouble. He could not let sleeping dogs lie as, perhaps, the elder man would have been glad to do. But in the postscript to this second letter there is the interesting assurance " I shall be all right in a few hours. It's impossible to depress me."

Despite religious squabbles, Stevenson was anything but unhappy in the autumn of 1873. In the summer he had gone to England to stay at a Suffolk rectory, " the house of a cousin of mine and of her husband, the delightful Churchill Babington," and in the rectory the man, always hungry for friendship, began one of the most fruitful friendships of his life. Among his fellow-guests was Mrs. Sitwell, who was afterwards to be Lady Colvin, a lady, Stevenson says, " whose generous pleasure—perhaps I might almost say whose weakness—it was to discover youthful genius." Sir Sidney Colvin has described his first meeting with Stevenson :

" I was shortly due to join the party, when Mrs. Sitwell wrote telling me of the ' fine young spirit ' she had found under her friend's roof, and suggesting that I should hasten my visit so as to make his acquaintance before he left. I came accordingly, and from that time on the fine young spirit became a leading interest both in her life and mine. He had thrown himself on her sympathies, in that troubled hour of his youth, with entire dependence almost from the first, and clung to her devotedly for the next two years as to an inspirer, consoler, and guide. Under her influence he began for the first time to see his way in life, and to believe hopefully and manfully in his own powers and future. To encourage such hopes further, and to lend what hand one could towards their fulfilment, became quickly one of the first cares and pleasures."

Stevenson confessed that he doubted whether Colvin, the Slade Professor at Cambridge, would have " taken to me by nature." It was Mrs. Sitwell's good opinion that gained him favour. " Meeting as we did, I the ready worshipper, he the ready patron, we had not got up the hill to the rectory before we had begun to make friends." Stevenson has paid fine tribute to his debt to Colvin :

" It is very hard for me, even if I were merely addressing the unborn, to say what I owe to and what I think of this most trusty and noble-minded man. If I am what I am and where I am, if I have done anything at all or done anything well, his is the credit. It was he who paved my way in letters ; it was he who set before me, kept before

me, and still, as I write, keeps before me, a difficult standard of achievement ; and it was to him
and to Fleeming Jenkin that I owed my safety at
the most difficult periods of my life. A friend of
one's own age is too easily pleased or too easily
silenced to be of much corrective use ; a friend
who is much our senior is too often a taskmaster
whom we serve with counterfeits and please with
falsehoods. These two had the tact and wisdom
to suffer me to be very much myself ; to accept
and cherish what was good in me ; to condone
much of what was evil ; and whilst still holding
before me a standard to which I could never quite
attain, neither to damp nor to disgust me of the
trial."

Colvin and Mrs. Sitwell accepted Stevenson as
a writer, and the letters that he began to write her,
as soon as he returned home, are full of his literary projects. He had completed the paper on
Roads, which was accepted by the editor of the
Portfolio, and was the first of his writing to be paid
for, and was busy with a study of Walt Whitman,
who had become the chief god of his idolatry.
His letters are full of unaffected gratitude, candid
self-revelation, and charming fancy. They, indeed, first reveal Stevenson's genius. I quote
one passage :

" It is a magnificent glimmering moonlight
night, with a wild, great west wind abroad, flap-
ping above one like an immense banner, and

every now and again swooping furiously against my windows. The wind is too strong perhaps, and the trees are certainly too leafless for much of that wide rustle that we both remember ; there is only a sharp, angry, sibilant hiss, like breath drawn with the strength of the elements through shut teeth, that one hears between the gusts only."

Almost in every year since the private publication of *The Pentland Rising* in 1866, Stevenson had completed some experimental work. *The Charity Bazaar, an Allegorical Dialogue,* was written in 1868 and first published in 1898. In the next year he wrote two poems and a paper called *A Retrospect.* One of the poems, *The Light-Keeper,* has remarkable colour and movement. It begins :

> The brilliant kernel of the night,
>   The flaming lightroom circles me :
> I sit within a blaze of light
>   Held high above the dusky sea.
> Far off the surf doth break and roar
> Along bleak miles of moonlit shore,
>   Where through the tides the tumbling wave
> Falls in an avalanche of foam
> And drives its churned waters home
>   Up many an undercliff and cave.

In 1871 Stevenson wrote five slight sketches ; in 1872 a paper on Cockermouth and Keswick, the *New Form of Intermittent Light for Lighthouses,* and six contributions to the short-lived *Edinburgh University Magazine.* One of them, *An Old Scots*

Gardener, from which I have quoted, was afterwards largely rewritten. Another, *The Philosophy of Umbrellas*, was written in collaboration with J. W. Ferrier, though, Stevenson says, " his principal collaboration was to lie back in an easy chair and laugh." It is a pleasant piece of rather obvious fooling, as may be gathered from the following extract :

" Robinson Crusoe presents us with a touching instance of the hankering after them inherent in the civilised and educated mind. To the superficial, the hot suns of Juan Fernandez may sufficiently account for his quaint choice of a luxury ; but surely one who had borne the hard labour of a seaman under the tropics for all these years could have supported an excursion after goats or a peaceful *constitutional* arm-in-arm with the nude Friday. No, it was not this : the memory of a vanished respectability called for some outward manifestation, and the result was—an umbrella. A pious castaway might have rigged up a belfry and solaced his Sunday mornings with the mimicry of church bells ; but Crusoe was rather a moralist than a pietist, and his leaf-umbrella is as fine an example of the civilised mind striving to express itself under adverse circumstances as we have ever met with."

In 1873, Stevenson wrote *Memories of Colinton Manse*, which has remained unpublished, but which obviously suggested *The Manse* in *Memories and Portraits*, a second scientific paper, *The Thermal Influence of Forests*, and the *Roads*.

In the October after his meeting with Colvin, Stevenson was ill with " a bad sore throat, fever, rheumatism and a threatening of pleurisy." It had been decided that he should be called to the English rather than to the Scottish Bar, but Sir Andrew Clark, who examined him on his arrival in London, ordered an immediate departure for the Riviera, and he left England on November 5th.

CHAPTER V

SCOTLAND AND FRANCE

IN his first weeks at Mentone, Stevenson read George Sand thoroughly—" I have found here a new friend to whom I grow daily more devoted," he wrote to Mrs. Sitwell—and Chateaubriand and " books on the French Calvinists which are necessary to my little Covenanting game." This interest in the Covenanters was still active, and perhaps was the reason why he found Chateaubriand " more antipathetic to me than any one else in the world." The Shorter Catechist could hardly be sympathetic to the famous apologist of the Catholic faith and the eulogist of Catholic worship.

At twenty-three Stevenson was already a conscious stylist. " It hurts me," he wrote to Mrs. Sitwell, " when neither words nor clauses fall into their places, much as it would hurt you to sing when you had a bad cold and your voice deceived you and missed every other note." He was writing a study of Walt Whitman, but his work did not satisfy him, and it is remarkable that so young a man should have been so severe a critic of himself. " Walt Whitman has stopped," he wrote,

" I have bemired it so atrociously by working at
it while I was out of humour that I must let the
colour dry." He suffered from the fits of depres-
sion natural to a man of high ambition and poor
health. " I have given up all hope, all fancy
rather, of making literature my hold : I see that
I have not capacity enough." But there is a
certain boyish insincerity in his complaints. " If
you knew how old I felt ! I am sure this is what
age brings with it—this carelessness, this dis-
enchantment, this continual bodily weariness."

His father had as usual been generous in the
supply of money, but Stevenson hated, or said he
hated, dependence. He wrote in one of his
letters : " It is an old phrase of mine that money
is the *atmosphere* of civilised life, and I do hate to
take the breath out of other people's nostrils. I
live here at the rate of more than £3 a week and
I do nothing for it. If I didn't hope to get well
and do good work yet and more than repay my
debts to the world, I should consider it right to
invest an extra franc or two in laudanum. But
I *will* repay it."

In *Lay Morals*, he wrote of " a friend of mine ;
a young man like others ; generous, flighty, as
variable as youth itself, but always with some high
notions, and on the search for higher thoughts of
life." The friend was of course R. L. S.

" Like many invalids, he supposed that he
would die. Now should he die, he saw no means

of repaying this huge loan which by the hands of his father, mankind had advanced him for his sickness. In that case it would be lost money. So he determined that the advance should be as small as possible ; and, so long as he continued to doubt his recovery, lived in an upper room, and grudged himself all but necessaries. But so soon as he began to perceive a change for the better, he felt justified in spending more freely, to speed and brighten his return to health, and trusted in the future to lend a help to mankind, as mankind, out of its treasury, had lent a help to him."

There was something of pretence in Stevenson's poverty, but there was something fine in his hatred of dependence.

Sidney Colvin joined him in Mentone at Christmas, and the coming of his friend had the most excellent effect on Stevenson's health and spirits. " I am less tired and dispirited than I was by a good way," he wrote to his mother. Colvin was obliged to go for a while to Paris, and while he was away Stevenson struck up an acquaintance with two Russian ladies, and the Shorter Catechist again reappears in his fear that one of them had designs on him. He confided his suspicions to Mrs. Sitwell : " I don't know what Mme. G.'s little game is with regard to me. Certainly she has either made up her mind to make a fool of me in a somewhat coarse manner, or else she is in train to make a fool of herself. I don't care which it is (though I sincerely hope the former) if it would only take a definite shape ; but in the meantime, I am damnably embarrassed and yet funnily interested." It is probable that these two very sophisticated women of the world were considerably amused by the romantic young Scotsman in his many gloomy moods. " *Monsieur*," said one of them, " *est un jeune homme que je ne comprends pas. Il n'est pas méchant, je sais cela, mais après, ténèbres, ténèbres, ténèbres, rien que des ténèbres.*"

He wrote of one of them, Madame Garschine :

> What is the face, the fairest face, till Care,
> Till Care the graver-Care with cunning hand,
> Etches content thereon and makes it fair,
> Or constancy, and love, and makes it grand ?

He was busy once more with his Walt Whitman and with the essay " Ordered South," which is included in the essays in *Virginibus Puerisque*. It is the plaint of a man who feels himself set apart from his fellows by the imminence of death. " The world is disenchanted for him. He seems to himself to touch things with muffled hands and to see them through a veil. His life becomes a palsied fumbling after notes that are silent when he has found and struck them. He cannot recognise that this phlegmatic and unimpressionable body with which he now goes burthened is the same that he knew heretofore so quick and delicate and alive."

Nearly twenty years later, Stevenson appended a qualifying note to his essay in which he suggests that as a man grows older, he acquires " a far higher notion of the blank that he will make by dying," and that realising the responsibilities and duties of life, he will, at the same time, realise that to die has " something of the air of a betrayal." Stevenson struggled with fine persistence to live, with the consciousness that it was always probable that he would soon die.   Years afterwards Mr. Lloyd Osbourne wrote :

" The truly dreadful part of his life was the uncertainty of its tenure ; the imminence always of a sudden death.   He would put a handkerchief to his lips, perceive a crimson stain, and then sooner or later there might be hemorrhage of the lungs, with all its horror and suspense, and its subsequent and unutterably dejecting aftermath of having to lie immovable for days and nights on end.   The mental agony was beyond expression ; one wonders how he ever bore up against it ; but the actual spells of illness were not extremely painful, nor were they as a rule very long continued.   The intervals between these hemorrhages lasted many months, and during these periods, except for the irksomeness of a confined life and the enforced separation from friends (whose rare visits tended to excite him and diminish his nervous force), he was on the whole exceedingly happy, and undisturbed by physical ills. His preoccupation for writing was so intense that in many ways he enjoyed this aloofness from the world. His time was not intruded on by a multitude of petty cares and petty engagements ; he could read and write and think—in peace ; he could let himself live in his stories without any jarring interruption."

The weather was cold, and Sidney Colvin brought Stevenson back from Paris a warm cloak " suited to his taste for the picturesque and piratical in apparel." The cloak gave Stevenson immense delight. He wrote to his father : " My cloak is the most admirable of all garments. For warmth unequalled ; for a sort of pensive, Roman stateliness, sometimes warming into Romantic guitarism, it is simply without concurrent ; it starts alone. If you could see me in my cloak, it would impress you. I am hugely better, I think." And in a letter to his mother he said : " It is a fine thought for absent parents that their son possesses simply THE GREATEST vestment in Mentone. It is great in size, and unspeakably great in design ; qua raiment, it has not its equal."

In February, at Mentone, Stevenson began his friendship with Andrew Lang. Lang admits that his first impression was not wholly favourable : " He looked as, in my eyes, he always did look, more like a lass than a lad, with a rather long smooth oval face, brown hair worn at greater length than is common, large lucid eyes, but whether blue or brown I cannot remember, if brown, certainly light brown. On appealing to the authority of a lady, I learn that brown *was* the hue. His colour was a trifle hectic, as is not unusual at Mentone, but he seems under his big blue cloak, to be of slender, yet agile frame. He was like nobody else whom I ever met. There was a sort of uncommon celerity in changing expression, in thought and speech. His cloak and Tyrolese hat (he would admit the innocent impeachment) were decidedly dear to him." [1] Stevenson found the older man rather overpoweringly donnish. It was a long time afterwards that he became the admired " Andrew with the brindled hair."

Colvin went back to England in March, and Stevenson followed him in April. Among other work that he had begun while in the South was a book to be called *Four Great Scotsmen*, to consist of studies of John Knox, David Hume, Robert Burns, and Walter Scott. He wrote to Mrs. Sitwell : " The Knox will really be new matter, as his life hitherto has been disgracefully written, and the events are romantic and rapid ; the character very strong, salient, and worthy ; much interest as to the future of Scotland, and as to that part of him which was truly modern under his Hebrew disguise. Hume, of course, the urbane, cheerful, gentlemanly, letter-writing

---

[1] *Adventures among Books*, by Andrew Lang, p. 43.

eighteenth century, full of attraction, and much that I don't yet know as to his work. Burns, the sentimental side that there is in most Scotsmen, his poor troubled existence, how far his poems were his personally, and how far national, the question of the framework of society in Scotland, and its fatal effects upon the finest natures. Scott again, the ever delightful man, sane, courageous, admirable ; the birth of Romance, in a dawn that was a sunset ; snobbery, conservatism, the wrong threat in History, and notably in that of his own land."

He had also begun the essay on Victor Hugo, which was published in the *Cornhill* in the following August. On his return to Edinburgh, Stevenson started to read seriously for the Bar. In the summer of '74 he stayed with Sidney Colvin at Hampstead, and was elected to the Savile Club.

The Savile Club was then at 15 Savile Row, from which it took its name. It was then, as it still is, the home of good talk and good fellowship, a place where the solemn bore is never quite happy. Sir Edmund Gosse, one of the most faithful as he was one of the most distinguished of the club members, has recalled a delightful incident in its history :

" In the front room Mr. Herbert Spencer was sitting at the fireplace, reading a book ; in the back room a young writer, already celebrated— whom I will not name, since he has left the club—

was regaling a circle of admirers with stories. At the close of each story there was a burst of laughter, at which Herbert Spencer lifted a pale face, tortured with disapprobation. At last a supreme story provoked in the back room a more explosive hilarity than ever. The philosopher, hurriedly feeling in his pockets, produced two padded ear-protectors ; these he clapped to the two sides of his head, and fixed them ; and then calmly resumed his book. There was a popular song in those days, ' The Old Obadiah and the Young Obadiah,' and this was an illustration of it." [1]

Sir Edmund continues :

" The conversations in the 'eighties in which the two Stevensons—R. L. S. and his wonderful cousin R. A. M. S.—took the predominant part, were not so vociferous nor so purely anecdotal. Day after day, these met at the luncheon-table with, to name only the dead, Andrew Lang, W. E. Henley, William Minto, H. J. Hood, sometimes Coventry Patmore and Austin Dobson. . . . The talk was not noisy when these men met in the absolute liberty of 15, Savile Row, but it was worthy of the finest traditions of eager, cultivated communication." [2]

It is a good thing to know that the tradition of fifty years ago still continues, including the annual party the boyish joy of which is unaffected by the " grandmotherly supervision of magistrate

[1] *Silhouettes*, Sir Edmund Gosse, p. 379.   [2] *Ibid.*, pp. 379-80.

or policeman," which Sir Edmund Gosse quite
properly resented.

In the autumn of 1874, Stevenson went for a
yachting tour in the western islands of Scotland,
and spent some weeks in the English countryside.
During this year he did a certain amount of
reviewing for the *Fortnightly Review*, and went on
with his *Walt Whitman* and the *Four Great Scotsmen*. " Knox and his females begin to get out
of restraint altogether," he wrote to Sidney Colvin.
The essay on Knox, which was finally entitled
John Knox and his Relations to Women, was printed
in *Macmillan's Magazine* in 1875. *Macmillan's* was
then edited by Sir George Grove, remembered
mainly for his exhaustive *Dictionary of Music*.
Stevenson remained highly critical of his work.
" I write so ill," he wrote in a letter to Mrs. Sitwell in November 1874, " so cheap and miserable
and penny-a-linerish is this *John Knox* that I have
just sent, that I am low."

In 1874, too, he wrote *An Appeal to the Clergy*—
it was published in pamphlet form in 1875—in
which he pleaded for the union of the Established
and Free Churches which has recently eventualised. This pamphlet, Sir Sidney Colvin says,
" attracted, I believe, no attention whatever."

The relations between Stevenson and his father
had grown much more pleasant. The older man
had ceased openly to resent his son's relapse from
orthodoxy, but Louis was miserable living in

Edinburgh, and the northern winter tried him
severely. He wrote to Mrs. Sitwell : " I have
discovered why I get on always so ill, and am
always so nasty, so much worse than myself, with
my parents ; it is because they always take me at
my worst, seek out my faults, and never give me
any credit. . . . O, I do hate this damned life that
I lead. Work—work—work ; that's all right,
it's amusing ; but I want women about me and
I want pleasure. John Knox had a better time
of it than I, with his godly females all leaving their
husbands to follow after him ; I would I were
John Knox ; I hate living like a hermit."

In the later weeks of 1874 he wrote his essay on
Poe, which was first published in the *Academy* in
1875. During the winter, Leslie Stephen, who
was then editing the *Cornhill*, took Stevenson with
him to the Edinburgh Infirmary, where W. E.
Henley was a patient. Henley was to be one
of the great figures in Stevenson's life Seven
years afterwards he wrote in the dedication to
Henley of *Virginibus Puerisque* : " What can be
more encouraging than to find the friend who
was welcome at one age, still welcome at another ?
. . . These papers are like milestones on the wayside of my life ; and as I look back in memory,
there is hardly a stage of that distance but I see
you present with advice, reproof, or praise."

Stevenson described the first meeting to Mrs.
Sitwell : " Yesterday, Leslie Stephen, who was

down here to lecture, called on me and took me up to see a poor fellow, a sort of poet who writes for him, and who has been eighteen months in our infirmary, and may be, for all I know, eighteen months more. It was very sad to see him there in a little room with two beds, and a couple of sick children in the other bed ; a girl came in to visit the children, and played dominoes on the counterpane with them ; the gas flared and crackled, the fire burned in a dull economical way ; Stephen and I sat on a couple of chairs, and the poor fellow sat up in his bed with his hair and beard all tangled, and talked as cheerfully as if he had been in a King's palace, or the great King's palace of the blue air. He has taught himself two languages since he has been lying there. I shall try to be of use to him."

The last sentence again suggests the Shorter Catechist. But for Henley his friend, as he knew him, was always the " riotous, intrepid, scornful Stevenson."

Henley's description of Stevenson remains the finest and most revealing thing ever written of him :

Thin-legged, thin-chested, slight unspeakably,
Neat-footed and weak-fingered : in his face—
Lean, large-boned, curved of beak, and touched with race,
Bold-lipped, rich-tinted, mutable as the sea,
The brown eyes radiant with vivacity—
There shines a brilliant and romantic grace,
A spirit intense and rare, with trace on trace

Of passion, impudence and energy.
Valiant in velvet, light in ragged luck,
Most vain, most generous, sternly critical,
Buffoon and poet, lover and sensualist :
A deal of Ariel, just a streak of Puck,
Much Antony, of Hamlet most of all,
And something of the Shorter-Catechist.

" Just a streak of Puck ! " If one were to search for a phrase that summarises Stevenson, could a better be found than the Presbyterian Puck ?

With Henley's portrait of Stevenson must always be read Stevenson's portrait of Henley :

" Burly is a man of great presence ; he commands a larger atmosphere, gives the impression of a grosser mass of character than most men. It has been said of him that his presence could be felt in a room you entered blindfold ; and the same, I think, has been said of other powerful constitutions condemned to much physical inaction. There is something boisterous and piratic in Burly's manner of talk which suits well enough with this impression. He will roar you down, he will bury his face in his hands, he will undergo passions of revolt and agony ; and meanwhile his attitude of mind is really both conciliatory and receptive ; and after Pistol has been out-Pistol'd, and the welkin rung for hours, you begin to perceive a certain subsidence in these spring torrents, points of agreement issue, and you end arm-in-arm, and in a glow of mutual admiration. The outcry only serves to make your final union the more unexpected and precious. Throughout there has been perfect sincerity, perfect intelligence, a desire to hear although not always to listen, and an unaffected eagerness to meet concessions."

Stevenson was an exile in his own land. His father had a circle of highly respectable friends who realised nothing of his son's brilliance. " Mostly they perceived little more than the exterior of the lad, with his dilapidated clothes, his long hair and distaste for office life," [1] says Sir Graham Balfour. The lad, it should be noted, was now a man of twenty-five, and the dilapidated clothes were the sheerest affectation. The capacity for self-pity remained. His mother was always devoted to him, but in a queer letter to Mrs. Sitwell he protested that he really wanted a French mother, not a Scottish. " My mother is my father's wife ; to have a French mother, there must be a French marriage ; the children of lovers are orphans."

Mr. Lloyd Osbourne says :

" France had a profound influence over Stevenson ; mentally he was half a Frenchman ; in taste, habits, and prepossessions he was almost wholly French. Not only did he speak French admirably and read it like his mother-tongue, but he loved both country and people, and was more really at home in France than anywhere else. Of course, like all Scotchmen, he had an inordin-

[1] *Life of R. L. Stevenson*, by Graham Balfour, vol. i. p. 121.

ate sentiment for his native land, but it was particularly a sentiment for the Scotland of the past —for the Scotland of history and romance, clanging with arms and resplendent in its heroic and affecting stories. Modern Scotland had less appeal, and though it held a very warm place in Stevenson's heart, he saw it always through that mist of bygone glory.

" What he praised most in the French as a national trait was their universal indulgence towards all sexual problems—their clear-sighted understanding and toleration of everything affecting the relations of men and women. He often said that in this the French were the most civilised people in Europe, and incomparably in advance of all others, ignoring as comparatively unimportant any criticism of their irritating bureaucracy, their lottery bonds, their grinding *octrois*, their window-taxes, and so on. Britain to his mind was an infinitely better governed country, but with an intellectual outlook, blinkered by caste, puritanism, and prejudice. He preferred France, with its mental and social freedom ; its frankness ; its lack of hypocrisy ; its democratic and kindly acceptance of life as it is. He often pointed out that once French culture had taken root it could never be obliterated. ' It has always conquered the conquerors,' he said. ' Get it started and it becomes ineradicable ' " [1]

[1] *New Arabian Nights*, Introd., pp. xx and xxi.

Stevenson was called to the Scottish Bar on July 14th, 1875. Sir Graham Balfour says that he actually received one brief, but he never seriously practised. Indeed, a fortnight after he was called he went with Sir Walter Simpson to France, staying at Fontainebleau, studying mediaeval French poetry, and collecting material for the admirable essay on Charles of Orleans, the unfortunate royal poet, who spent years a prisoner in the Tower of London. This essay was published in the *Cornhill Magazine* in December 1876, and the smug study of François Villon appeared in the same magazine in 1887. Barbizon and its artist society greatly influenced Stevenson. He wrote of the artist colony in his essay *Memories of Fontainebleau* :

" The lads are mostly fools ; they hold the latest orthodoxy in its crudeness ; they are at that stage of education, for the most part, when a man is too much occupied with style to be aware of the necessity for any matter ; and this, above all for the Englishman, is excellent. To work grossly at the trade, to forget sentiment, to think of his material and nothing else, is, for a while at least, the king's highway of progress. Here, in England, too, many painters and writers dwell, dispersed, unshielded, among the intelligent bourgeois. These, when they are not merely indifferent, prate to him about the lofty aims and moral influence of art. And this is the lad's ruin. For art is, first of all and last of all, a trade. The love of words and not a desire to publish new discoveries, the love of form and not a novel reading of historical events, mark the vocation of the writer and the painter. The arabesque, properly speaking, and even in literature, is the first fancy of the artist ; he first plays with his material as a child plays with a kaleidoscope ; and he is already in a second stage when he begins to use his pretty counters for the end of representation. In that, he must pause long and toil faithfully ; that is his apprenticeship ; and it is only the few who will really grow beyond it, and go forward, fully equipped, to do the business of real art—to give life to abstractions and significance and charm to facts. In the meanwhile, let him dwell much among his fellow-craftsmen. They alone can take a serious interest in the childish tasks and pitiful successes of these years. They alone can behold with equanimity this fingering of the dumb keyboard, this polishing of empty sentences, this dull and literal painting of dull and insignificant subjects. Outsiders will spur him on. They will say, ' Why do you not write a great book ? paint a great picture ? ' If his guardian angel fail him, they may even persuade him to the attempt, and, ten to one, his hand is coarsened and his style falsified for life."

In his letters during this French holiday with Walter Simpson, and after he had returned to Edinburgh, there are two extracts that show that

death was never for long out of his mind   The
first is a paraphrase of Bainville :

> *Nous n'irons plus au bois.*
> We 'll walk the woods no more,
> But stay beside the fire,
> To weep for old desire
> And things that are no more.
>   The woods are spoiled and hoar,
>   The ways are full of mire ;
>   We 'll walk the woods no more,
>   But stay beside the fire,
>   We loved, in days of yore,
>   Love, laughter, and the lyre,
>   Ah God, but death is dire,
>   And death is at the door—
>   We 'll walk the woods no more.

The second is in a letter written to Mrs. Sitwell
from Scotland : " I cannot tell how I feel, who
can ever ? I feel like a person in a novel of
George Sand's ; I feel I desire to go out of the
house, and begin life anew in the cool blue
of night ; never to come back here ; never,
never."

Stevenson remained at home through the
winter of 1875 and until the summer of 1876.
He had been commissioned to write the article on
Burns for the *Encyclopaedia Britannica*, but it was
regarded as too critical and was never printed.
An article on Béranger however, a very colour-
less production, was afterwards commissioned and
accepted. He was busy, too, with the essays in
Virginibus Puerisque, many of which, as is common

with the work of young writers, suffered many rejections.

In the autumn of 1876 he went on the canoe adventure with Sir Walter Simpson which he has described in *An Inland Voyage*.

CHAPTER VI

THE ROMANCE OF FONTAINEBLEAU

STEVENSON'S inland voyage began at Antwerp and finished at Grez-sur-Loing on the borders of the forest of Fontainebleau, but he and his companion, Sir Walter Simpson, did not canoe all the way. The story of the adventure was Stevenson's first published book, and for it, according to Mrs. Stevenson, he received twenty pounds from the publishers. Stevenson never wrote anything more charming than his first book, a volume of unusual travel and amusing adventure and of suggestive and characteristic reflections. In the early summer he had been reading fifteenth-century French literature with " Boswell daily by way of a Bible," and he carried the poems of Charles of Orleans with him in his canoe, the *Arethusa*.

The voyage was a sufficiently hazardous undertaking. " For my part," he wrote, " I had never been in a canoe under sail in my life ; and my first experiment out in the middle of this big river (the Scheldt) was not made without some trepidation." During the voyage Stevenson was frequently wet through, which must have been particularly bad for a man of his ill-health, and once he was nearly drowned. He wrote to Henley :

" I have been wet through nearly every day of travel since the second ; besides this, I have had to fight against pretty mouldy health ; so that, on the whole, the essayist and reviewer has shown, I think, some pluck. Four days ago I was not a hundred miles from being miserably drowned, to the immense regret of a large circle of friends and the permanent impoverishment of British Essayism and Reviewery. My boat cul-butted me under a fallen tree in a very rapid current : and I was a good while before I got on to the outside of that fallen tree ; rather a better while than I cared about. When I got up, I lay some time on my belly, lanting, and exuded fluid. All my symptoms *jusqu'ici* are trifling. But I 've a damned sore throat."

The *Inland Voyage* is a completely entertaining record because Stevenson loved it all, the perils and the wettings—" the discomfort when it is honestly uncomfortable and makes no nauseous pretensions to the contrary is a vastly humorous business "—the kindly help of the rowing men of Brussels and the hospitality of the *juge de paix* at Landrecies, the good food and drink in the good inns, and the occasional snubbing from a cur-mudgeon of an inn-keeper, even the arrest at Châtillon-sur-l'Oise. The very names of the towns were a joy. Well, indeed, may he be envied who meets no fewer than four attractive sisters at Origny-Sainte-Benoîte ! As for the arrest, who can blame a Commissary of Police for regarding a man, dressed as Stevenson was dressed, with some suspicion. " On his head, he wore a smoking-cap of Indian work, the gold lace pitifully frayed and tarnished. A flannel shirt of an agreeable dark hue, which the satirical called black ; a light tweed coat made by a good English tailor ; ready-made cheap linen trousers and leathern gaiters completed his array. In person, he is exceptionally lean ; and his face is not like those of happier mortals, a certificate."

With his delightful felicity of phrase, Stevenson possessed the power of acute observation and appreciation. There is a fine passage in the *Inland Voyage* of " the smell of many trees," which illustrates this combination of gifts.

Always it was Robert Louis Stevenson who most interested the voyager. It is not the least of his attractions that he was the unashamed egoist. " If people," he wrote, " knew what an inspiring thing it is to hear a man boasting, so long as he boasts of what he really has, I believe they would do it more freely and with a better grace." Robert Louis Stevenson was the more determined to enjoy Robert Louis Stevenson for fear that he might not enjoy him very long : " For I think we may look upon our little private war with death

somewhat in this light. If a man knows he will
sooner or later be robbed upon a journey, he will
have a bottle of the best in every inn, and look
upon all his extravagances as so much gained upon
the thieves. And above all, where, instead of
simply spending, he makes a profitable invest-
ment for some of his money, when it will be out of
risk of loss. So every bit of brisk living, and above
all when it is healthful, is just so much gained upon
the wholesale filcher, death. We shall have the
less in our pockets, the more in our stomachs,
when he cries, ' Stand and deliver.' "

The Shorter Catechist, even though he were
disguised in " a smoking-cap of Indian work," is
revealed in the references to the religion of the
country, and Stevenson himself realised that " a
Protestant born and bred," and particularly, it
must be added, born and bred in Edinburgh, can
never, except by grace, understand Catholicism.
But even the Catholic can sympathise with the
reflection inspired by the Cathedral at Noyon :

" I could never fathom how a man dares to lift
up his voice to preach in a cathedral. What is
he to say that will not be an anti-climax? For
though I have heard a considerable variety of
sermons, I never yet heard one that was so ex-
pressive as a cathedral. 'Tis the best preacher
itself, and preaches day and night ; not only
telling you of man's art and aspirations in the
past, but convincing your own soul of ardent

sympathies ; or rather, like all good preachers, it sets you preaching to yourself,—and every man is his own doctor of divinity in the last resort."

Stevenson tired of the voyage before it was over, but it gave him many good things to remember. " The lamps were lighted and the salads were being made in Origny-Sainte-Benoîte by the river." And he was itching to write. " O for a room with a table and to sit down to work," he wrote to his mother. For him, its ending is the best of every adventure. "You may paddle all day long ; it is when you come back at nightfall and look in at the familiar room that you find Love or Death awaiting you beside the stove ; and the most beautiful adventures are not those we go to seek."

A new and greater adventure awaited Stevenson at Grez, which he and his cousin already knew well, and where they were vastly popular in the society of " all races of artistic men."

The year before, an American lady had landed in Antwerp with her three small children. Fanny Lloyd Osbourne was born in Indianapolis in 1840. She was thus ten years older than the man who was to be her second husband. Mrs. Osbourne had married when she was a girl of seventeen and had settled in California. Her marriage was unfortunate. Her husband was notoriously unfaithful, but her sister says that " divorce was at that time a far more serious step than it is now, and for the sake of her family she hesitated long before taking it."[1] However, living with her husband became intolerable and, with a very thin purse, Mrs. Osbourne came to Europe to secure a measure of freedom. From Antwerp the family went to Paris, where the mother and her daughter studied art. " We were miserably poor,"[2] Mr. Lloyd Osbourne, the elder son, has recorded. The younger boy was taken ill and died. His mother was heartbroken and herself very ill, and she was advised by a friendly American artist to go for a while to Grez. The hotel, Siron's, was an artists' monopoly, and few women had ever stayed there. But Mrs. Osbourne and her daughter had singular charm and were first tolerated and then welcomed. Mrs. Osbourne has been described by an American writer as " slight with delicately moulded features and vivid eyes gleaming from under a mass of dark hair," and another of her compatriots has said : " Mrs. Osbourne was in no sense ordinary. Indeed, she was gifted with a mysterious sort of over-intelligence, which is almost impossible to describe, but which impressed itself upon every one who came within the radius of her influence. . . . She was therefore both physically and mentally the very antithesis of the gay, hilarious, open-minded and open-hearted Stevenson, and for

---

[1] *Life of Mrs. R. L. Stevenson*, by N. V. de G. Sanchez, p. 41.
[2] *New Arabian Nights*, Introd., p. ix.
[3] *Life of Mrs. R. L. Stevenson*, by N. V. de G. Sanchez, p. 50.

that very reason perhaps the woman in all the world best fitted to be his life comrade and help-mate. At any rate we may well ask ourselves if anywhere else he would have found the kind of understanding and devotion which she gave him from the day of their first meeting at Grez until the day of his death in far-away Samoa." [1] In later years, Richard Le Gallienne wrote of " her splendid leonine head, her great hypnotic eyes and her overwhelming magnetism." [2]

R. A. M. Stevenson was awaiting Stevenson at Grez, and had already made friends with the Osbournes, who had heard much of Louis from his admiring cousin. At last he appeared. Mr. Lloyd Osbourne has described the scene : " Then in the dusk of a summer's day as we all sat at dinner about the long *table d'hôte*, some sixteen or eighteen people, of whom my mother and sister were the only women and I the only child, there was a startling sound at one of the open windows giving on the street, and in vaulted a young man with a dusty knapsack on his back. The whole company rose in an uproar of delight, mobbing the newcomer with outstretched hands and cries of greeting. He was borne to a chair ; was made to sit down in state, and still laughing and talk-ing in the general hubbub was introduced to my mother and sister."

[1] *Life of Mrs. R. L. Stevenson*, by N. V. de G. Sanchez, p. 51.
[2] *The Romantic '90's*, by Richard Le Gallienne, p. 83.

Mr. Osbourne protests that Stevenson's long
hair and peculiar clothes were no mere affecta-
tions, but were the consequence of his straitened
means. But Stevenson had always exaggerated
the straitened means, and he certainly at this
time was receiving an adequate allowance from
his father. He shared, indeed, the pleasant affectation of his age and his class. The smoking-cap
with the gold lace was a protest against respectability and its intention was to *épater la bourgeoisie.*
Mr. Lloyd Osbourne indeed admits : " All these
lads—for they were scarcely more—were gloriously
under the spell of the *Vie de Bohème* ; they wanted
to be poor, improvident and reckless ; they were
eager to assert that they were outcasts and rebels."
From their first meeting Lloyd Osbourne became a hero-worshipper. He has recalled
Stevenson as he first saw him : " He was tall,
straight, and well-formed, with a fine ruddy com-
plexion, clustering light-brown hair, a small
tawny moustache, and extraordinarily brilliant
brown eyes. But these details convey nothing of
the peculiar sense of power that seemed to radiate
from him—of a peculiar intensity of character that
while not exactly dominating had in its quality
something infinitely more subtle and winning ;
and he was besides, so sparkling, so easily the
master in all exchange of talk and raillery that I
gazed at him in spell-bound admiration." [1]

[1] *New Arabian Nights*, Introd., p. xii.

Stevenson fell in love with Mrs. Osbourne at first sight. He wrote verses for her, he played with her children, he was soon " Luly " to them. The friendship was continued in Paris, with a return to the forest of Fontainebleau in the two summers that followed. In the autumn of 1878 the Osbournes were obliged to return to America. For the moment, any idea of marriage was impossible. Mrs. Osbourne was still tied, Stevenson's earnings were still small, and Sir Graham Balfour says he could hardly expect his parents " to give their assistance or even their consent to the marriage." [1] There is no reference to Mrs. Osbourne in the published letters, but there is a new note of seriousness in them.

Stevenson was in Edinburgh in 1877, but he spent the greater part of the year in France, at Paris and at Fontainebleau. In the spring of 1878 he stayed for a while at Burford Bridge, near Dorking, where he met George Meredith, for whom he had an enthusiastic admiration, and from there he went to Paris as private secretary to Professor Fleeming Jenkin, his old Edinburgh professor, who was a juror at the Paris Exhibition. It was while he held this position—the only regular work he ever had—that he said good-bye to Mrs. Osbourne. His literary work included a certain amount of reviewing—he severely slated a poem of Browning's—and the essays collected

[1] *Life of R. L. Stevenson*, by Graham Balfour, vol. i., p. 157.

in *Virginibus Puerisque* and *An Inland Voyage*, which was published in 1878. He also wrote his first stories—*A Lodging for the Night*, *The Sire de Malétroit's Door*, and *Will o' the Mill*. *The New Arabian Nights* and *Providence and the Guitar* appeared in *London*, edited by Henley, and *Picturesque Notes on Edinburgh* in the *Portfolio*.

Stevenson's mood is reflected in a letter that he wrote to his father from Paris in February 1878 :

CAFÉ DE LA SOURCE, BD. ST. MICHEL,
PARIS, 15*th Feb.* 1878.

" The Wisdom of this world consists in making oneself very little in order to avoid many knocks ; in preferring others, in order that, even when we lose, we shall find some pleasure in the event ; in putting our desires outside of ourselves, in another ship, so to speak, so that, when the worst happens, there will be something left. You see, I speak of it as a doctrine of life, and as a wisdom for this world. People must be themselves, I suppose. I feel every day as if religion had a greater interest for me ; but that interest is still centred on the little rough-and-tumble world in which our fortunes are cast for the moment. I cannot transfer my interests, not even my religious interests, to any different sphere. . . .

" I have had some sharp lessons and some very acute sufferings in these last seven-and-twenty years—more even than you would guess. I begin to grow an old man ; a little sharp, I fear, and a little close and unfriendly ; but still I have a good heart, and believe in myself and my fellow-men and the God who made us all. . . . There are not many sadder people in this world, perhaps, than I. . . . There is a fine text in the Bible, I don't know where, to the effect that all things work together for good to those who love the Lord. Strange as it may seem to you, everything has been, in one way or the other, bringing me a little nearer to what I think you would like me to be. 'Tis a strange world, indeed, but there is a manifest God for those who care to look for him. . . . *P.S.* While I am writing gravely, let me say one word more. I have taken a step towards more intimate relations with you. But don't expect too much of me. Try to take me as I am. This is a rare moment, and I have profited by it ; but take it as a rare moment. Usually I hate to speak of what I really feel, to that extent that when I find myself *cornered*, I have a tendency to say the reverse."

His father had some reason to complain that he received little news of his son's doings, but, on the whole, the relations between them had become cordial and understanding. Stevenson was never much of a playgoer—his one attempt at theatrical criticism was a failure—but he went a good deal to the theatre in Paris in these days, and in a letter to Mrs. Sitwell in 1878 he said : " There is only one very good thing in the world : the acting of Sarah Bernhardt." He read Racine and Anthony Trollope. Of Trollope he wrote : " He is so nearly wearying you and yet he never does ; or rather he never does until he gets near the end when he begins to wean you from him so that you are as pleased to be done with him as you thought you would be sorry." He professed, too, an odd admiration for Samuel Richardson. But perhaps that was a Quartier Latin joke. It was to a correspondent in far-away Australia that he wrote :

" Please, if you have not, and I don't suppose you have, already read it, institute a search in all Melbourne for one of the rarest and certainly one of the best of books—*Clarissa Harlowe.* For any man who takes an interest in the problems of the two sexes, that book is a perfect mine of documents. And it is written, sir, with the pen of an angel. Miss Howe and Lovelace, words cannot tell how good they are ! And the scene where Clarissa beards her family, with her fan going all the while ; and some of the quarrel scenes between her and Lovelace ; and the scene where Colonel Marden goes to Mr. Hall, with Lord M. trying to compose matters, and the Colonel with his eternal ' finest woman in the world,' and the inimitable affirmation of Mobray—nothing, nothing could be better ! You will bless me when you read it for this recommendation ; but, indeed, I can do nothing but recommend *Clarissa.*

I am like that Frenchman of the eighteenth century who discovered Habakkuk, and would give no one peace about that respectable Hebrew. For my part, I never was able to get over his eminently respectable name ; Isaiah is the boy, if you must have a prophet, no less. About *Clarissa*, I meditate a choice work : *A Dialogue on Man, Woman, and 'Clarissa Harlowe.'* It is to be so clever that no array of terms can give you any idea ; and very likely that particular array in which I shall finally embody it, less than any other."

He had now grown eager to get a greater vitality into his work. Style was not enough. He wrote to Mrs. Sitwell : " Vividness and not style is now my line ; style is all very well, but vividness is the real line of country ; if a thing is meant to be read, it seems just as well to try and make it readable."

An Inland Voyage was favourably reviewed, much, so he professed, to Stevenson's astonishment. He wrote to his mother from Paris : " About criticisms, I was more surprised at the tone of the critics than I suppose any one else. And the effect it has produced in me is one of shame. If they liked that so much, I ought to have given them something better, that 's all. And I shall try to do so. Still, it strikes me as odd ; and I don't understand the vogue. It should sell the thing."

Stevenson was frequently in London on his way from Edinburgh to Paris, and most of his time was spent at the Savile Club. It was in 1877 that he became on terms of intimate friendship with Edmund Gosse. Sir Edmund has written : " A childlike mirth leaped and danced in him ; he seemed to skip upon the hills of life. He was simply bubbling with quips and jests ; his inherent earnestness or passion about abstract things was incessantly relieved by jocosity ; and when he had built one of his intellectual castles in the sand, a wave of humour was certain to sweep in and destroy it. I cannot, for the life of me, recall any of his jokes ; and written down in cold blood, they might not be funny if I did. They were not wit so much as humanity, the many-sided outlook upon life. I am anxious that his laughter-loving mood should not be forgotten, because later on it was partly, but I think never wholly, quenched by ill-health, responsibility and the advance of years. He was often, in the old days, excessively and delightfully silly—silly with the silliness of an inspired schoolboy ; and I am afraid that our laughter sometimes sounded ill in the ears of age." [1]

Twelve years afterwards, in one of the early chapters of *The Wrecker*, Stevenson recalled his Paris days, specifically recording that his poverty was pretence : " I dined, I say, at a poor restaurant and lived in a poor hotel ; and this was

[1] *Critical Kit-Kats*, by Edmund Gosse, pp. 279, 280.

not from need, but sentiment. My father gave me a profuse allowance, and I might have lived (had I chosen) in the Quartier de l'Etoile and driven to my studies daily. Had I done so, the glamour must have fled : I should still have been but Loudon Dodd ; whereas now I was a Latin Quarter student, Murger's successor, living in flesh and blood the life of one of those romances I had loved to read, to re-read, and to dream over, among the woods of Muskegon. . . . The most grievous part was the eating and drinking. I was born with a dainty tooth and a palate for wine ; and only a genuine devotion to romance could have supported me under the cat-civets that I had to swallow, and the red ink of Bercy I must wash them down withal. Every now and again, after a hard day at the studio, where I was steadily and far from unsuccessfully industrious, a wave of distaste would overbear me ; I would slink away from my haunts and companions, indemnify myself for weeks of self-denial with fine wines and dainty dishes ; seated perhaps on a terrace, perhaps in an arbour in a garden, with a volume of one of my favourite authors propped open in front of me, and now consulted awhile, and now forgotten :—so remain, relishing my situation, till night fell and the lights of the city kindled ; and thence stroll homeward by the riverside, under the moon or stars, in a heaven of poetry and digestion."

After he had finished his engagement with Fleeming Jenkin in 1878, Stevenson went from Paris to La Monastier on the Loire. He had planned a second canoe voyage with Walter Simpson. This was prevented for some reason or the other, and on September 23rd, Stevenson set out with his donkey Modestine for the eleven days' tramp through the Cevennes. He was restless and unhappy, and Mrs. Osbourne, from whom he had just parted, was always in his mind. In his *Travels with a Donkey* he wrote : " I heard the voice of a woman singing some sad, old, endless ballad not far off. It seemed to be about love and a *bel amoureux*, her handsome sweetheart ; and I wished I could have taken up the strain and answered her, as I went on upon my invisible woodland way, weaving, like Pippa in the poem, my own thoughts with hers. What could I have told her ? Little enough ; and yet all the heart requires. How the world gives and takes away, and brings sweethearts near, only to separate them again, into distant and strange lands ; but to love is the great amulet which makes the world a garden ; and ' hope which comes to all,' outwears the accidents of life, and reaches with tremulous hand beyond the grave and death. Easy to say : yea, but also, by God's mercy, both easy and grateful to believe."

The *Travels with a Donkey* were written in the winter of 1878-79 and published in the following

June. He says in the Dedication to Sidney
Colvin : " But we are all travellers in what John
Bunyan calls the wilderness of this world—all, too,
travellers with a donkey ; and the best that we
find in our travels is an honest friend. He is a
fortunate voyager who finds many. We travel,
indeed, to find them. They are the end and the
reward of life. They keep us worthy of ourselves ;
and, when we are alone, we are only nearer to
the absent." [1]

Ferdinand Fabre is the novelist of the Cevennes,
and Sir Edmund Gosse has noted :

" An English writer, of higher rank than Fabre,
was revealing the Cevennes to English readers
just when the Frenchman was publishing his
mountain stories. If we have been reading *Le
Chevrier*, it will be found amusing to take up again
Through the Cevennes with a Donkey of Robert Louis
Stevenson. The route which the Scotchman took
was from Le Monastier to Alais, across the north-
eastern portion of the mountain-range, while
Fabre almost exclusively haunts the south-western
slopes in Hérault. Stevenson brings before us a
bleak and stubborn landscape, far less genial than
the wooded uplands of Bédarieux. But in both
pictures much is alike. The bare moors on the
tops of the Cevennes are the same in each case,
and when we read Stevenson's rhapsody on the
view from the high ridge of the Mimerte, it might

[1] *Travels with a Donkey*, p. 129.

well be a page translated from one of the novels of Ferdinand Fabre." [1]

Kegan Paul, the publishers of *An Inland Voyage*, published the *Travels with a Donkey*, again paying the author twenty pounds. Mrs. Stevenson says : " Kegan Paul not only paid twenty pounds for the *Travels with a Donkey*, but invited the author to dinner, where the shy young man suffered agonies of embarrassment over the claret that was served to the guests alone, Mr. Paul being an abstainer from principle. Would the acceptance, at his invitation, of the wine Mr. Paul thought it wrong to take, put Mr. Paul in a false position ? And yet, on what grounds to refuse ? This delicate question became so harassing to the Scotch conscience, that, as my husband has told me, he would have infinitely preferred to dine not at all."

It was characteristic of him, and incidentally proof of the unreality of his money troubles, that he should write to his mother : "The book is out. I have given away all my copies and bought £20 worth besides."

Stevenson sent Henley his poem *Our Lady of the Snows*, suggested to him by the Trappist monastery in the Cevennes, and Henley apparently sharply criticised its construction, and particularly the lines :

My undissuaded heart I hear
Whisper courage in my ear.

And Stevenson replied in semi-comic protest.

[1] *French Profiles*, Sir Edmund Gosse, p. 174.

Stevenson spent many weeks in 1878 and the early part of 1879 in London, collaborating with Henley in *Deacon Brodie*, the first of the plays which they wrote together, and Sir Graham Balfour says that he was offered and refused a position as leader writer on the staff of the *Times*. He was in Edinburgh in the summer. He had bad news of Mrs. Osbourne's health and happiness. He felt that he could stay no longer away from her, and on August 7th he sailed from the Clyde for New York in the steamship *Devonia*.

CHAPTER VII

THE COVENANTER MARRIED

STEVENSON, says Sir Sidney Colvin, made the journey from Scotland to California " in the steerage and the emigrant train." Stevenson himself has said : " I was not in truth a steerage passenger. Although anxious to see the worst of emigrant life, I had some work to finish on the voyage and was advised to go by the second cabin where at least I should have a table at hand."

The difference in fare was only two pounds, and the difference in comfort was inconsiderable. Sir Sidney Colvin says that Stevenson set out on this adventure " to test his power of supporting himself and eventually others by his own labours in literature." As a matter of fact he dashed half across the world because he was a young man very much in love. He was obliged to economise, because he knew that his father would strongly disapprove his intention and would almost certainly refuse to supply funds, and he welcomed the new, if somewhat uncomfortable experience with its novel associations, because he was a born adventurer and a born journalist who smelt copy in the steerage. Incidentally, it amused him to play the amateur emigrant. Stevenson never tired of play-acting, and he was quite content that he should be the only member of his audience. Mrs. Stevenson says that he once told her son, " I am Don Quixote." It was a pleasant and a harmless pretence. His wife goes on : " Too much ease frightened him ; he would occasionally insist on some sharp discomfort such as sleeping on a mat on the floor or dining on a ship's biscuit, to awaken him, as he said, to realities." All just play-acting, the rather pathetic play-acting of a sick man !

The story of the voyage to America is told in the first part of *The Amateur Emigrant*, written immediately on his arrival. Stevenson arranged for its publication, but it was withdrawn at the earnest wish of his father—the well-to-do father is never long absent—and it was not actually published, and then in a considerably abridged form, until 1895. When Sir Sidney Colvin read the first draft, it seemed to him " compared to his previous travel papers a somewhat wordy and spiritless record of squalid experiences." The description is entirely justified. There is in *The Amateur Emigrant* none of the charm and the spontaneity of *An Inland Voyage* or *Travels with a Donkey*. It is " copy," not literature.

During the voyage to America, Stevenson finished *The Story of a Lie*, written " in a slantindicular cabin with the table playing bob-cherry

H

with the ink bottle." It appeared in the *New Quarterly Magazine* in October 1879. *The Story of a Lie* is a thin novelette, autobiographical in some of its details. " When Dick Naseby was in Paris," it begins, " he made some odd acquaintances for he was of those who have ears to hear and can use their eyes no less than their intelligence. . . . He was a type-hunter among mankind." The theme of the story is a quarrel between father and son. Stevenson knew, of course, that his sudden trip to America would anger his father as much as his apparent lapse from the Shorter Catechism. There is therefore genuine personal significance in the sentence in his story : " Dick had a respect for his father as the best of men, tempered by the politic revolt of a youth who has to see his own independence."

Stevenson landed in New York on August 18th, and started west in the emigrant train on the following day. His land journey was described in *Across the Plains*, now the second part of *The Amateur Emigrant*, most of which was first printed in various magazines, including *Fraser's*, *Longman's*, and *Scribner's*, in the years from 1883 to 1888. Stevenson wrote to Sir Sidney Colvin of *The Amateur Emigrant* : " I have sought to be prosaic in view of the nature of the subject," and he afterwards described the book not unfairly as " a pretty heavy emphatic piece of pedantry." But he believed it was what the public wanted. *Across the Plains* is, however, far less prosaic than *From the Clyde to Sandy Hook*.

Stevenson was ill when he landed in New York. Bad food, bad air and hard work had brought him down. The train journey tried him severely. " My body is all to whistles," he wrote to Henley, and the trip across America was only made endurable by frequent doses of laudanum.

Mrs. Lloyd Osbourne and her son were living in the old Mexican town of Monterey. " It was Mexico's last stronghold," Mrs. Osbourne had written, and Stevenson has said :

" The town, when I was there, was a place of two or three streets, economically paved with seasand, and two or three lanes, which were watercourses in the rainy season, and were, at all times, rent up by fissures four or five feet deep. There were no street lights. Short sections of wooden sidewalk only added to the dangers of the night, for they were often high above the level of the roadway, and no one could tell where they would be likely to begin or end. The houses were, for the most part, built of unbaked adobe brick, many of them old for so new a country, some of very elegant proportions, with low, spacious shapely rooms, and walls so thick that the heat of summer never dried them to the heart. At the approach of the rainy season a deathly chill and a graveyard smell began to hang about the lower floors ; and diseases of the chest are common and fatal among house-keeping people of either sex."

Stevenson was a sorry figure when he arrived at Monterey. "He looked ill even to my childish gaze," says Lloyd Osbourne. The brilliancy of his eyes emphasised the thinness and pallor of his face; his clothes, no longer picturesque but merely shabby, hung loosely on his shrunken body, and there was about him an indescribable lessening of his alertness. He was miserably lodged and had his meals at "a grubby little restaurant" which in after years he recalled with some pleasure. He continued to write with feverish zest. "It is the dibbs that are wanted," he wrote to Henley, and *The Pavilion on the Links*, "grand carpentry story in nine chapters," was sent to England in October. "At times," he wrote, "I get terribly frightened about my work, which seems to advance too slowly. I hope soon to have a greater burthen to support, and must make money a great deal quicker than I used." Mrs. Osbourne, indeed, had arranged for her divorce, and their marriage was at last made possible.

But busy and worried as he was, Stevenson still found time to play the fool. Among his escapades at Monterey was the denunciation of the Spanish priest for his rapacity, and setting fire to the forest, "for which had I been caught, I should have been hung out of hand to the nearest tree."

Before the end of October, Stevenson was left alone. His health was still very bad. " I am somewhat of a mossy ruin," he wrote to P. G. Hamerton. In the early part of December he was ill with pleurisy : " This pleurisy," he said, in a letter to Edmund Gosse, " though but a slight affair in itself was a huge disappointment to me and marked an epoch. To start a pleurisy about nothing while leading a dull regular life in a mild climate was not my habit in past days." He was feverishly eager to earn money. He was full of plans for the future, and was working on, among other things, a novel called *The Vendetta in the West*, which was never finished. Before Christmas he was in San Francisco, lonely and discouraged : " I must own that the guts are a little knocked out of me." His friends in London were extremely critical of the writing that he had sent home, and he was still earning considerably less than two hundred a year. " Everybody writes me sermons," he wrote to Sidney Colvin, " it 's good for me, but hardly the food necessary for a man who lives all alone on forty-five cents a day." Incidentally he was obviously sincerely grieved by his estrangement from his father : " I please myself with hoping that my father will not always think so badly of my conduct nor so very slightingly of my affection as he does at the present." But his anxieties did not affect his industry. Among his work in the early weeks of 1880 was the essay *Yoshida-Torajiro*, an admirable piece of work, and the essay on *Thoreau*, which is even better.

Yoshida, the Japanese patriot, attracted him by his courage and persistence. "It is exhilarating," he wrote, "to have lived in the same days with these great-hearted gentlemen. Only a few miles from us, to speak by the proportion of the universe, while I was droning over my lessons, Yoshida was goading himself to be wakeful with the stings of the mosquito ; and while you were grudging a penny income tax, Kusákabé was stepping to death with a noble sentence on his lips."

The analysis of Thoreau is very acute. He was something of a prig and a skulker. "He did not wish virtue to go out of him among his fellow-men, but slunk into a corner to hoard it for himself. He left all for the sake of certain virtuous self-indulgences." And Stevenson comments : "A man who must separate himself from his neighbours' habits in order to be happy, is in much the same case with one who requires to take opium for the same purpose. What we want to see is one who can breast into the world, do a man's work, and still preserve his first and pure enjoyment of existence."

There was no sort of affinity between the two men. Stevenson depended on his friends and gloried in the dependence. Thoreau wrote :

" We have nothing to fear from our foes ; God keeps a standing army for that service ; but we have no ally against our Friends, those ruthless Vandals." For the writer Stevenson expresses critical admiration : " Whatever Thoreau tried to do was tried in fair, square prose, with sentences solidly built, and no help from bastard rhythms."

In March he was again dangerously ill. He wrote to Edmund Gosse :

" I have been very sick ; on the verge of a galloping consumption, cold sweats, prostrating attacks of cough, sinking fits in which I lost the power of speech, fever, and all the ugliest circumstances of the disease : and I have cause to bless God, my wife that is to be, and one Dr. Bamford (a name the Muse repels), that I have come out of all this, and got my feet once more upon a little hilltop, with a fair prospect of life and some new desire of living. Yet I did not wish to die, neither ; only I felt unable to go on farther with that rough horseplay of human life : a man must be pretty well to take the business in good part. Yet I felt all the time that I had done nothing to entitle me to an honourable discharge ; that I had taken up many obligations and begun many friendships which I had no right to put away from me ; and that for me to die was to play the cur and slinking sybarite, and desert the colours on the eve of the decisive fight."

His father heard of the straits in which his son

was placed, probably from one of his English friends, and in May, Stevenson received a cable saying that he could count on an allowance of two hundred and fifty pounds a year. By this time Mrs. Osbourne had obtained her divorce, and with the assurance of this small certain income she and Stevenson were married on May 19th. " Marriage," Stevenson once wrote, " is of so much use to a woman ; opens out to her so much more of life and puts her in the way of so much more freedom and usefulness that whether she marry ill or well, she can hardly miss some benefit." This is a delightfully masculine point of view, and certainly, when she married for the second time, the benefit for Mrs. Stevenson must have seemed somewhat problematical. Still, her daughter had married Austin Strong a few weeks before, and Mrs. Stevenson had only her one son to think of, and although his health was precarious, by his marriage to her Stevenson protected her from ever again being penniless. He had contributed to the Widows' Fund of the Scottish Bar since the time he was called in 1872, and actually from his death in 1894 to her death his widow received an annuity from the fund.

The wedding was not a particularly joyous occasion. The bridegroom was a very sick man. " I am beyond a doubt greatly stronger," he wrote, " and yet still useless for any work and I may say for any pleasure." He was, as he has described himself, " a mere complication of cough and bones, much fitter for an emblem of mortality than a bridegroom." Mrs. Osbourne had no illusion. Her biographer says : " She married him when his fortunes both in health and finances were at their lowest ebb, and she took this step in the almost certain conviction that in a few months at least she would be a widow. The best that she hoped for was to make his last days as comfortable and as happy as possible." [1] He wrote in *Virginibus Puerisque* :

" You may safely go to school with hope ; but ere you marry, should have learned the mingled lesson of the world ; that dolls are stuffed with sawdust, and yet are excellent playthings ; that hope and love address themselves to a perfection never realised, and yet, firmly held, become the salt and staff of life ; that you yourself are compacted of infirmities, perfect, you might say, in imperfection, and yet you have a something in you lovable and worth preserving ; and that, while the mass of mankind lies under this scurvy condemnation, you will scarce find one but, by some generous reading, will become to you a lesson, a model, and a noble spouse through life. So thinking, you will constantly support your own unworthiness, and easily forgive the failings of your friend. Nay, you will be wisely glad that you retain the sense of blemishes ; for the faults

[1] *Life of Mrs. R. L. Stevenson*, by N. V. de G. Sanchez, p. 77.

of married people continually spur up each of them, hour by hour, to do better and to meet love upon a higher ground. And ever, between the failures, there will come glimpses of kind virtues to encourage and console."

Immediately after their marriage, the Stevensons, with young Lloyd Osbourne, went up into the mountains to a half-ruined mining camp which he has described in *The Silverado Squatters*, where Stevenson read Hazlitt and wrote for four or five hours a day.

They were " in a land of stage drivers and highwaymen, a land in that sense like England a hundred years ago," a land, therefore, immensely interesting to Stevenson who, soon after his arrival in the mountains, had his first talk on the telephone. " So it goes in these new countries ; telephones and telegraphs and newspapers and advertisements running far ahead among the Indians and the grizzly bears."

They " squatted " in a house of three rooms and " so plastered against the hill that one room was right atop of another, that the upper floor was twice as large as the lower, and all three apartments must be entered from a different side and level." The squatters were Stevenson, his wife, and his stepson, and " a setter crossed with spaniel," called Chu-chu," who was entirely unsuited for a rough life. He had been brought up softly, and Stevenson says : " It may seem hard to say of a dog that Chu-chu was a tame cat."

The mountain air had the best effect on his health. He became, as he said, " a married and convalescent being." Their stay in the mountains was saddened by the fact that Mrs. Stevenson and her son fell ill with diphtheria, but unquestionably the clear air saved Stevenson's life. In July Mrs. Stevenson wrote to her mother-in-law, whom she had never seen : " As to my dear boy's appearance, he improves every day in the most wonderful way, so that I fancy by the time you see him you will hardly know that he has ever been ill at all. I do try to take care of him ; the old doctor insists that my nursing saved him ; I cannot quite think it myself, as I shouldn't have known what to do without the doctor's advice, but even having it said is a pleasure to me. Taking care of Louis is, as you must know, very like angling for shy trout ; one must understand when to pay out the line, and exercise the greatest caution in drawing him in. I am becoming most expert, though it is an anxious business. I do not believe that any of Louis's friends, outside of his own family, have ever realized how very low he has been ; letters followed him continually, imploring, almost demanding his immediate return to England, when the least fatigue, the shortest journey, might, and probably would, have proved fatal ; and, which at the moment filled my heart

with bitterness against them, they actually asked
for work. Now, at last, I think he may venture
to make the journey without fear, though every
step must be made cautiously. I am sure now
that he is on the high road to recovery and health,
and I believe his best medicine will be the meeting with you and his father, for whom he pines
like a child. I have had a sad time through it all,
but it has been worse for you, I know. I am now
able to say that all things are for the best. Louis
has come out of this illness a better man than he
was before ; not that I did not think him good
always, but the atmosphere of the valley of the
shadow is purifying to a true soul ; and though he
may be no nearer your hearts than before, I believe you will take more comfort in your son than
you have ever done." [1]

His father and mother were now very anxious
that he should return home. His wife was convinced that he could stand the journey, and on
the 7th August they sailed from New York. It
was the anniversary of the day on which he had
sailed from Glasgow.

Stevenson's was one of those rare marriages
that can be written down unqualified successes.
" I think my marriage was the best move I ever
made in my life," he wrote, and there can be no
question that his wife not only kept him alive,
but that her influence made him a far finer writer

[1] *Life of Mrs. R. L. Stevenson*, by N. V. de G. Sanchez, pp. 79, 80.

than he would have been without her. She had,
as Sir Sidney Colvin has said, " a character as
strong, interesting and romantic almost as Stevenson's own." His love for her gave him a purpose
in his life, and as their association went on, he
became less and less a *poseur* and more and more
a Shorter Catechist.

In the year of their marriage Stevenson's wife
was forty and already a grandmother, and only
eleven years younger than his mother. Stevenson
has paid charming tribute to his wife in one of his
Songs of Travel :

MY WIFE

Trusty, dusky, vivid, true,
With eyes of gold and bramble-dew,
Steel-true and blade-straight,
The great artificer
  Made my mate.

Honour, anger, valour, fire ;
A love that life could never tire,
Death quench or evil stir,
The mighty master
  Gave to her.

Teacher, tender, comrade, wife,
A fellow-farer true through life,
Heart-whole and soul-free,
The august father
  Gave to me.

Stevenson had gone to America to marry.
Having married, his heart ached for Scotland,

and he was eager enough to obey the parental invitation.   He has written :

" There is no special loveliness in that grey country, with its rainy, sea-beat archipelago ; its fields of dark mountains ; its unsightly places, black with coal ; its treeless, sour, unfriendly looking cornlands ; its quaint, grey, castled city, where the bells clash of a Sunday, and the wind squalls, and the salt showers fly and beat.   I do not even know if I desire to live there ; but let me hear, in some far land, a kindred voice sing out, ' O why left I my hame ? ' and it seems at once as if no beauty under the kind heavens, and no society of the wise and good, can repay me for my absence from my country.   And though I think I would rather die elsewhere, yet in my heart of hearts I long to be buried among good Scots clods."

Stevenson's father met him and his wife and stepson at Liverpool, and they went together to Scotland, first to Blair Athol and afterwards to Strathpeffer, where they stayed until the middle of September.   Mrs. Stevenson made an immediate conquest of her mother-in-law and father-in-law.   Between old Mr. Stevenson and herself there were many points of similarity, and as their acquaintance became more intimate, he began more and more to appreciate her judgment.   It was his son's judgment that Thomas Stevenson most distrusted, and he urged him " never to

publish anything without Fanny's approval."
Certainly Fanny did everything possible to please,
even wearing white stockings because old Stevenson thought there was something slightly improper
in black stockings.

At Strathpeffer, Stevenson, fresh from California, was thrilled, more than he had ever been
before, by the beauty of his native land. " Near
here is a valley," he wrote to Colvin, " birch
woods, heather and a stream ; I have lain down
and died ; no country, no place was ever for a
moment so delightful to my soul. And I have
been a Scotsman all my life and denied my native
land ! Away with your gardens of roses, indeed !
Give me the cool breath of Rogie waterfall, hence-
forth and for ever, world without end."

He met Principal Tulloch at Strathpeffer, and
planned the writing of a history of the Highlands
and the Clans, one of many literary projects that
never eventualised.

But he was ill all through the summer. He
suffered from " acute chronic catarrh accompanied by disquieting lung symptoms and great
weakness," and it was clear that a Scottish winter
would kill him. It was accordingly arranged
that he should spend the winter in Davos, which
was just beginning its fame as a sanatorium for
sufferers with lung trouble, and on October 7th
he left Edinburgh, with his wife and stepson and
Woggs, the black Skye terrier which was to be an

important member of the family for the next six years. They stayed for a day or two at the Grosvenor Hotel in London. " I am terrified at this hotel," wrote Stevenson, " but I hope to-morrow we get to Paris where I know how to live cheap and well."

The journey to Davos fifty years ago was a wearisome adventure, entailing an eight hours' coach journey up the valley of the Prattigau. Stevenson carried with him a letter of introduction to John Addington Symonds who, handicapped much in the same way as Stevenson, was kept alive for fifteen or sixteen years by the Alpine air and the Alpine sunshine. The friendship with the elder literary man was the chief pleasure of Stevenson's winter. " I like Symonds very well though he is, I think, much of an invalid in mind and character," he wrote to Colvin. " But his mind is interesting with many beautiful corners, and his consumptive smile very winning to see."

Stevenson did very little work at Davos. He read a great deal for the Highland history which he discussed in many of his letters. He wrote his essays *Samuel Pepys* and *The Morality of the Profession of Letters*, and some of the essays which were collected in *Underwoods*. Edmund Gosse was arranging a collection of English odes for Kegan Paul, and in a letter written to him on December 19th, Stevenson, who had discussed the book with Symonds, made certain suggestions which afford an interesting indication of his literary taste. He was emphatic for Shelley's *The World's Great Age*, Herrick's *Meddowes* and *Come, my Corinna*, Milton's *Time* and *Solemn Music*, *The Greek Phase*, and particularly Tennyson's *The Duke of Wellington*. " We will have the Duke of Wellington, by God."

There is a singularly illuminative passage in a long letter written from Davos to his mother, in which Stevenson is again revealed as both Cavalier and Catechist. He wrote on the day after Christmas 1880 :

" I wonder if you or my father ever thought of the obscurities that lie upon human duty from the negative form in which the ten commandments are stated ; or of how Christ was so continually substituting affirmatives. ' Thou shalt not ' is but an example : ' Thou shalt ' is the law of God. It was this that seems meant in the phrase that ' not one jot or tittle of the law should pass.' But what led me to the remark is this : A kind of black angry look goes with that statement of the law in negatives. ' To love one's neighbour as oneself ' is certainly much harder, but states life so much more actively, gladly, and kindly, that you can begin to see some pleasure in it ; and till you can see pleasure in these hard choices and bitter necessities, where is there any Good News to men ? It is much more important to do right than not to do wrong ; further, the

I

one is possible, the other has always been and will ever be impossible ; and the faithful *desire to do right* is accepted by God : that seems to me to be the gospel, and that was how Christ delivered us from the law. After people are told that surely they might hear more encouraging sermons. To blow the trumpet for good would seem the parson's business ; and since it is not in our own strength, but by faith and perseverance (no account made of slips) that we are to run the race, I do not see where they get the material for their gloomy discourses. Faith is, not to believe the Bible, but to believe in God ; if you believe in God (or, for it 's the same thing, have that assurance you speak about) where is there any more room for terror ? "

Davos did not do Stevenson much good—" I have lost weight, pulse, respiration, etc., and gained nothing in the way of my old bellows "— and the place did not agree with his wife, whose heart was affected by living in a high altitude, and who found it depressing " to live with a dying and suffering people all about you." In his essay, *The Stimulation of the Alps*, Stevenson wrote that the frame of mind of the invalid upon the Alps is a sort of intermittent youth with periods of lassitude, and he complained that " the mountains are about you like a trap."

Moreover, Stevenson hated staying very long in one place, and with the coming of spring his wife, with her memories of California, yearned for warmth and colour. " I cannot deny that living here is living in a well of desolation," she wrote to her mother-in-law. They left Davos at the end of April, making a short stay in Paris on their road home to Scotland. " A week in Paris," Stevenson said, " reduced me to the limpness and lack of appetite peculiar to a kid glove and gave Fanny a jumping sore throat."

During this winter Thomas Stevenson must indeed have been more generous than ever, for his son's earnings were of the slightest. Lloyd Osbourne was left at school in France, and Stevenson and his wife were back in Edinburgh on May 30th.

CHAPTER VIII

THE CROWN OF SUCCESS

IN June the Stevensons were settled in a cottage at Pitlochry. This cottage in the Highlands was all that Stevenson's Scottish soul demanded. Within a few yards was " a little green glen with a burn—a wonderful burn, gold and green and snow white, singing loud and low in different steps of its career, now pouring over miniature crags, now fretting itself to death in a maze of rocky stairs and pots ; never was so sweet a little river. Behind, great purple moorlands reaching to Ben Vrackie." [1] But the weather was cold and wet. Mrs. Stevenson says : " My husband, who had come to the Highlands solely for the sunshine and bracing air, was condemned to spend the most of the time in our small, stuffy sitting-room, with no amusement or occupation other than that afforded by his writing materials. The only books we had with us were two large volumes of the life of Voltaire, which did not tend to raise our already depressed spirits." [2]

There are in Stevenson's letters at this time many indications of his insatiable curiosity and

---

[1] *The Merrie Men*, Preface, p. xi. [2] *Ibid.*, p. xii.

his interest in comparatively unimportant historical personages. At Pitlochry he was eager for information concerning Jean Cavalier, the Protestant leader in the Cevennes, of whom he had learned during his travels with a donkey. At the same time, he was spluttering with rage at the literary style of the revisers of the Bible—the Revised Version had just been published—whom he denounced as " loathsome literary lepers." Mrs. Stevenson says that her husband's writing at Pitlochry was " only for our mutual entertainment," a curious statement in view of their insistent need of money. He planned this summer a series of Tales of Terror which he called Crawlers. Of these he wrote *Thrawn Janet*, his first essay in the Scottish vernacular, which he told Sidney Colvin " frightened him to death," but which, as a matter of fact, has no very great power or distinction. Sir Graham Balfour believes that " the fame of Stevenson as a novelist is inseparably connected with his mastery over the common tongue of his own country," [1] but the English reader will always be puzzled and sometimes irritated by the language of the kailyard. It is, perhaps, truer to say that Stevenson gained fame as a novelist, despite his constant use of " the common tongue of his own country." At Pitlochry, too, he wrote *The Merrie Men*. Sir Graham Balfour says that *The Merrie Men* was

[1] *Life of R. L. Stevenson*, by Graham Balfour, vol. i. p. 189.

always one of his favourites, but Mrs. Stevenson
says that it "never quite satisfied its author, who
believed that he had succeeded in giving the
terror of the sea but had failed to get a real grip
of his story." [1] Most of his readers will agree
with him.

While he was at Pitlochry, Stevenson heard
that Professor Mackay had resigned the professorship of History and Constitutional Law in the
University of Edinburgh. All that the Professorship entailed was the delivery of a course of lectures during the summer term, and the stipend
was £200 a year. The election was in the hands
of the Edinburgh Faculty of Advocates and, with
the smallest academic qualifications, Stevenson
determined to stand as a candidate. He wrote
to Sidney Colvin : "I do believe I can make
something out of it. It will be a pulpit in a sense ;
for I am nothing if not moral, as you know." He
got busy at once collecting testimonials from
Leslie Stephen, J. A. Symonds, Andrew Lang,
Edmund Gosse, George Meredith, and others.
"Testimonial hunting is a queer form of sport,"
he wrote, "but it has its pleasures." Having
applied for a Professorship, Stevenson imagined
himself a Professor and amused himself by de-
livering long lectures on constitutional history,
to which his wife and stepson, who had again
joined the family, were obliged to listen. His

---

[1] *The Merrie Men*, Preface, p. xiii.

candidature was never really serious, and at the
election, despite the testimonials, he only received three votes.

Stevenson was very ill in July. In August the
family removed to Braemar, and here in " the
late Miss M'Gregor's cottage " he began to write
his *Treasure Island*. Mr. Chesterton declares
that the writing of *Treasure Island* is an historic
event. The story, says Mr. Chesterton, was " a
protest against the theory that pessimism is another name for culture." But to prove his theory,
Mr. Chesterton has mixed his dates. Certainly
Samuel Butler's *Erewhon* and James Thomson's
The City of Dreadful Night were published years
before *Treasure Island* was written. But the age
of pessimism had not yet begun. Oscar Wilde
was still unknown, Mr. Wells who, Mr. Chesterton
says, was " prophesying that the outline of history would end not in communism but in canni-
balism," was a boy of fifteen, and his first book
was not to be published for another fourteen years.
And the " Yellow Book " era was nearly a decade
ahead. Mr. Chesterton believes that Stevenson
wrote *Treasure Island* because of " his growing
sense of the need of some escape from the suffocating cynicism of the mass of men and artists in
his time." [1] He did nothing of the sort. He
wrote *Treasure Island* to amuse a small boy whom
he loved, who was cooped up in the late Miss

[1] *Stevenson*, by G. K. Chesterton, p. 107.

M'Gregor's cottage during a very wet August. In amusing the small boy, he vastly amused himself and, incidentally, found his real place in literature. However much Stevenson may have owed to his wife, his debt to his stepson, Lloyd Osbourne, was almost as great. What small boy ever did a finer deed than to inspire *Treasure Island*?

Of course *Treasure Island* is well written. Stevenson was a master stylist who could not write badly ; and, of course, it was something of a shock to the dull and cultured to find a literary artist writing a penny dreadful. " It was as if Paderewski had insisted on only going round with a barrel-organ," says Mr. Chesterton, " or Whistler had confined himself solely to painting public-house signs." [1] But if Whistler had painted public-house signs, they would have had all Whistler's qualities. So with *Treasure Island* and Robert Louis Stevenson.

The book began with the map. Young Lloyd Osbourne was drawing a map on a dull wet afternoon, and his stepfather helped him. Mr. Osbourne has told the story : " I shall never forget the thrill of Skeleton Island, Spy-Glass Hill, nor the heart-stirring climax of the three red crosses ! And the greater climax still when he wrote down the words ' Treasure Island ' at the top right-hand corner ! And he seemed to know

[1] *Stevenson*, by G. K. Chesterton, p. 102.

so much about it too—the pirates, the buried
treasure, the man who had been marooned on the
island. ' Oh, for a story about it,' I exclaimed,
in a heaven of enchantment, and somehow conscious of his own enthusiasm in the idea." [1] The
next day Lloyd Osbourne was called to Stevenson's bedroom to hear the first chapter of *Treasure
Island*. Fifteen chapters were written in Braemar,
several in Weybridge, and the novel, which was
first called *The Sea Cook*, was finished in Davos.
The early chapters of *Treasure Island* delighted
Lloyd Osbourne. They delighted Stevenson.
They delighted his father and, fortunately, they
delighted Dr. Alexander Japp, a new friend who
had come to Braemar to discuss Thoreau.
Through Dr. Japp's influence the serial rights
were sold to *Young Folks*. "The terms were
£2. 10s. a page of 450 words," Stevenson wrote
to Henley, "that's not noble, is it? But I have
my copyright safe. I don't get illustrated—a
blessing." It should be added that both Edmund
Gosse and Sidney Colvin praised *Treasure Island*,
and neither was generally addicted to the penny
dreadful.

Before he had left Braemar, and the story was
only at its beginning, Stevenson was already planning other work on the same lines, among them a
highwayman story to be called *Jerry Abershaw :
A Tale of Putney Heath*.

[1] *Treasure Island*, Preface, p. xviii.

There is really nothing in the least strange in the writing of *Treasure Island*. There is nothing in the least incongruous in a man who had read Balzac, and lived in the Quartier Latin and was a literary purist, writing a story of dashing adventure from which women and love were quite properly eliminated. It was the most natural thing in the world for Stevenson to write *Treasure Island*. It was the one of his books that he could not help writing. All his life he loved dressing up. But he did not always want to dress up in the same disguise. All his life he loved adventure. He possessed, indeed, all the spiritual qualities necessary for the successful writer of romance. Despite the Covenanter's blood in his veins, and the Covenanter's prejudice in his soul, he was never really a mystic. Neither in *Thrawn Janet* nor in the later *Dr. Jekyll and Mr. Hyde* did he suggest the power of creating horror, which is the mark of the genius of Edgar Allan Poe. It was movement, colour, romance, pretence, perhaps, that he loved. With *Treasure Island*, Stevenson found himself and found his market. Incidentally he achieved what had long been his ambition—he wrote a successful novel. " Although I had attempted the thing with rigour not less than ten or twelve times, I had not yet written a novel," he wrote. " All— all my pretty ones—had gone for a little and then stopped inexorably, like a schoolboy's watch. I might be compared to a cricketer of many years' standing who should never have made a run." [1]

The character of John Silver, one of the few characters in modern fiction that one remembers as one remembers Becky and Sam Weller, was suggested by Henley—and Henley was not very flattered. In his essay *My First Book*, Stevenson wrote : " I had an idea for John Silver from which I promised myself funds of entertainment : to take an admired friend of mine (whom the reader very likely knows and admires as much as I do), to deprive him of all his finer qualities and higher graces of temperament, to leave him with nothing but his strength, his courage, his quickness, and his magnificent geniality, and to try to express these in terms of the culture of a raw tarpaulin, such physical surgery is, I think, a common way of ' making character ' ; perhaps it is, indeed, the only way."

Happy in the work of writing a story for a child, Stevenson also, while he was at Braemar, began to write the poems afterwards collected in *A Child's Garden of Verses*. When the volume was published, it was dedicated to his old nurse, and Mrs. Stevenson says that " every poem in *The Child's Garden* was a bit out of his own childhood."

Treasure Island was written to please one boy, and has pleased a wilderness of boys. *A Child's Garden* was written to please the same boy, but I am not sure that it has much appeal to ordinary

[1] *Treasure Island*, Preface, p. xxiv.

boys and girls. In the envoy, To my Mother,
Stevenson wrote :

> You too, my mother, read my rhymes
> For love of unforgotten times,
> And you may chance to hear once more
> The little feet along the floor.

Without doubt, both to nurse and mother, the
poems brought back " the little feet along the
floor." But they are too sophisticated and too
sentimental for nursery popularity. Most men
remember the incidents of their youth. Few
men remember how the incidents affected them
at the time. It is common enough for events to
be remembered. It is a rare gift to be able to
recall moods. So childish sorrow and childish
joy are both constantly misrepresented both in
grown-up gossip and writing. In the first part of
David Copperfield, Dickens actually records a child's
experiences as a child felt them, an almost unique
achievement. Stevenson knew how to interest
and enthrall children. He had forgotten, as most
of us forget, how a child thinks. Take for example the poem, *Where Go the Boats ?* :

> Dark brown is the river,
>   Golden is the sand.
> It flows along for ever,
>   With trees on either hand.
>
> Green leaves a-floating,
>   Castles of the foam,
> Boats of mine a-boating—
>   Where will all come home ?

On goes the river
And out past the mill,
Away down the valley,
Away down the hill.

Away down the river,
A hundred miles or more,
Other little children
Shall bring my boats ashore.

This is a poem of disillusionment. No child can be disillusioned. It is the acceptance of the fact that Tom will reap what Harry has sown. But Harry must be a horrid little prig if he believes that it is right and proper that Tom shall pick his flowers.

Before the end of September the weather at Braemar became unendurable, and after a short stay in London and at Weybridge, the Stevensons were back again in Davos in October. John Addington Symonds was apparently horrified that any man, who could write, should write *Treasure Island*. He tried to persuade Stevenson to put away such foolish things. "In his ardour to academicise Stevenson, and make him classically respectable," says Mr. Lloyd Osbourne, "he even ferreted out a scarcely known Greek author and suggested that R. L. S. should collate all the scraps of information about him and write a ' Life.' " [1]

Treasure Island was by no means Stevenson's

[1] *Treasure Island*, Preface, p. xiii.

only preoccupation at Davos. He planned the Life of Hazlitt, which was never written. He was busy with the proofs of *Familiar Studies*. He discussed with Edmund Gosse a scheme for re-telling " in choice literary form " the most picturesque recent murder cases. He finished *The Silverado Squatters*. During the winter he wrote some 35,000 words. He generally worked fairly steadily for four or five hours a day. But, despite *Treasure Island*, he was restless and unsatisfied. " I work, work, work away and get nothing or very little done," he wrote to his mother. " It 's slow, slow, slow." And in a letter to Sidney Colvin, he said : " I brought home with me from my bad times in America two strains of unsoundness of mind, the first a perpetual fear that I can do no more work—the second a perpetual fear that my friends have quarrelled with me." The poem, *The Celestial Surgeon*, which begins :

> If I have faltered more or less
> In my great task of happiness,

was written in Davos, and probably accurately expresses the poet's mood.

His own health was better in this second winter in the Alps, but his wife again suffered a good deal from the high altitude. In December she went to Zurich, Stevenson fetching her home for Christmas. He described the journey in a letter to his mother : " Yesterday, Sunday and Christmas, we finished this eventful journey by a drive

in an *open* sleigh—none others were to be had—
seven hours on end through whole forests of Christmas trees. The cold was beyond belief. I have
often suffered less at a dentist's." Mrs. Stevenson
was more or less ill until they left Davos.

Stevenson loved dressing up, and he loved playing with toys. In his own inimitably suggestive
manner Mr. Chesterton has made much of this
love for toy theatres, and, in Davos, Stevenson and
Lloyd Osbourne had vast amusement from a tiny
press on which they produced two small books.
These little productions, now most rare and valuable, were sold at sixpence each. Their principal
attraction was the blocks, which Stevenson himself
made. Mr. Lloyd Osbourne has described the
making :

" Louis, who was a man of infinite resourceful-
ness (he could paint better theatre-scenes than any
one could buy), said that he would try to carve
some pictures on squares of fretwood. The word
fretwood seems as unknown nowadays as the thing
itself ; it was an extremely thin piece of board
with which one was supposed to make works of
art with the help of pasted-on patterns, an aggra-
vating little saw, and the patience of Job. . . .
Well, Louis cut out a small square of fretwood,
and in a deeply-thoughtful manner applied himself to the task. He had only a pocket-knife ;
real tools came later ; but he was impelled by a
will to win that carried all before it.

" After an afternoon of almost suffocating ex-
citement—for the publisher—he completed the
engraving that accompanies the poem : ' Reader,
your soul upraise to see.' But it had yet to be
mounted on a wooden block in order to raise it to
the exact level of the type. At last this was done.
A proof was run off. But the impression was unequal. Oh the disappointment ! Author and
publisher gazed at each other in misery. But
woman's wit came to the rescue. Why not build
it up with cigarette-papers ? ' Bravo, Fanny ! '
The author set to work, deftly and skilfully. Then
more proofs, more cigarette-papers, more running
up and down stairs to the little boy's room, which
in temperature hovered about zero. But what
was temperature ? The thing was a success." [1]

In addition to this publishing enterprise,
Stevenson painted scenery for his stepson's cardboard theatre, and together they played a peculiar
form of *Kriegspiel*, which Mr. Lloyd Osbourne has
also described : " The attic floor was made into
a map, with mountains, towns, rivers, ' good '
and ' bad ' roads, bridges, morasses, etc. Four
soldiers constituted a ' regiment,' with the right
to one shot when within a certain distance of
the enemy ; and their march was twelve inches
a day without heavy artillery, and four inches
with heavy artillery. Food and munitions were
condensed in the single form of printers' ' M's '.

[1] *Poems*, vol. i., Prefatory Note, pp. 175-6.

twenty to a cart, drawn by a single horseman, whose move, like that of all cavalry, was the double of the infantry. One ' M ' was expended for every simple shot ; four ' M's ' for every artillery shot—which returned to the base to be again brought up in carts. The simple shots were pellets from spring-pistols ; the artillery shots were the repeated throws of a deadly double sleeve-link.

" Here absurdity promptly entered, and would certainly have disturbed a German staff-officer. Some of our soldiers were much sturdier than others and never fell as readily ; on the other hand there were some dishearteningly thin warriors that would go down in dozens if you hardly looked at them ; and I remember some very chubby and expensive cavalrymen from the Palais Royal whom no pellets could spill. Stevenson excelled with the pistol, while I was crack shot with the sleeve-link. The leader who first moved his men, no matter how few, into the firing-range was entitled to the first shot. If you had thirty regiments you had thirty shots ; but your opponent was entitled to as many return shots as he had regiments, regardless of how many you had slaughtered in the meanwhile." [1]

Whether it was work or play, whatever Stevenson did, he did with a will, and whatever he did, he did with distinction.

[1] *Treasure Island*, Preface, p. xiv.

K

Stevenson unquestionably gained a good deal from his two stays in Davos, but the improvement in his own health was overbalanced by his constant anxiety for his wife, who always had to pay, and they left the Alps in April with very considerable relief. The summer of 1882 was unlucky and comparatively sterile. Stevenson stayed for a while at Burford Bridge, where he again met George Meredith, whose *Egoist* he had read for the first time in Davos, and whom he has described as " the only man of genius of my acquaintance." At the end of May they were back again in Scotland, stopping at a manse in Peeblesshire. " It is low, damp, and *mauchy*," he wrote to Henley. " The rain it raineth every day." His health was again very bad, and his fears for the future were accentuated by the news that Symonds was growing steadily worse.

There is a letter written during this year that indicates Stevenson's persistent love of the pulpit. To a young man who had written to him in some perplexity concerning the writings of Walt Whitman, he said : " If you can make it convenient to be chaste, for God's sake avoid the primness of your virtue ; hardness to a poor harlot is a sin lower than the ugliest unchastity."

Stevenson had planned to stay in Britanny at the end of the summer, but it was decided that it would be advisable for him to return to the Provence which he loved, and in September he went with his cousin, R. A. M. Stevenson, to Montpelier. Here, however, his chest trouble returned, and he moved to Marseilles, where his wife joined him, and where they settled in a house in a suburb of the city. But Stevenson remained very ill with continual hemorrhages, and was far too weak to attempt any work. An outbreak of typhus in the village added to their troubles, and, ill as he was, Mrs. Stevenson made up her mind to send him to Nice. Here his health quickly mended. After a short stay they went to Hyères and settled in a cottage, the Chalet La Solitude, " with a garden like a fairy story and a view like a classical landscape," where they lived for nine months, and where Sir Graham Balfour says Stevenson found " a greater happiness than ever came to him again." " The weather is incredible," he wrote to Colvin in February 1883, " my heart sings, my health satisfies even my wife." " I am in excellent health and write from four to five hours a day," he wrote to Mrs. Sitwell.

The Hyères chalet inspired the poem :

> My wife and I, in one romantic cot,
> The world forgetting, by the world forgot,
> High as the gods upon Olympus dwell,
> Pleased with the things we have, and pleased as well
> To wait in hope for those which we have not.
> She vows in ardour for a horse to trot ;
> I pledge my votive powers upon a yacht ;
> Which shall be first remembered, who can tell—
> My wife or I ?

Harvests of flowers o'er all ou r garden-plot,
She dreams ; and I to enricl a darker spot,—
My unprovided cellar ; both to swell
Our narrow cottage huge as a hotel,
That portly friends may cou e and share our lot—
My wife and I.

1883 was a very busy year. *A Child's Garden of Verses* was seen through the press. *The Silverado Squatters* was sold for American publication to the Century Company. *Treasure Island* was published in book form by Cassells, the author receiving a hundred pounds advance, and the second thriller, *The Black Arrow*, was written and serialised in *Young Folks*. But the main work of the year was the writing of *Prince Otto*. " My head is singing with Otto," he wrote to Henley in April. . . . " The thing travels and I like it when I am at it." And in another letter he wrote :

" *Otto* is, as you say, not a thing to extend my public on. It is queer and a little, little bit free ; and some of the parties are immoral ; and the whole thing is not a romance, nor yet a comedy ; but a kind of preparation of some of the elements of all three in a glass jar. I think it is not without merit, but I am not always on the level of my argument, and some parts are false, and much of the rest is thin ; it is more a triumph for myself than anything else ; for I see, beyond it, better stuff. I have nine chapters ready, or almost ready, for press."

For the first time in his life Stevenson was

almost self-support ng. At the end of the year
he recorded the r ceipt of £465 and an addi-
tional £250 due tc him from various publishers.
Treasure Island bro ght him something like fame.
The reviewers wei e enthusiastic. Andrew Lang
wrote : " I do no know except *Tom Sawyer* and
the *Odyssey* that I (ver liked any romance so well."
But during the fi st year only 5600 copies were
sold, a small en ugh sale compared with the
achievement of n odern " best sellers." Stevenson had for yeai ; longed to be self-supporting,
but now that he was beginning really to make
money, he also l egan to be bored by his own
success. " I don t like trying to support myself,"
he told Henley. " I hate the strain and the
anxiety, and whe a unexpected expenses are foisted
on me, I feel the world is playing with false dice."
But this hardly ings true.

His work w s becoming as well known in
America as in] ngland. In this year American
editions were p iblished of the *Arabian Nights* and
An Inland Voya ;e, and copies were sent to the
author by " s(me repentant publishers," from
whose piracy l e had apparently previously suffered. But 1883 had its anxiety and its sorrow
as well as its success. Stevenson was greatly
troubled by his father's health. In September he
was saddened by the news of the death of Walter
Ferrier, the oldest of his friends, except his cousin
Robert. " He was the only gentle one of all my

friends," Stevenson wrote to Henley. "To think that he was young with me, sharing that weather-beaten, Fergussonian youth, looking forward through the clouds to the sun-burst ; and now clean gone from my path, silent—well, well. This has been a strange awakening. Last night, when I was alone in the house, with the window open on the lovely still night, I could have sworn he was in the room with me ; I could show you the spot ; and, what was very curious, I heard his rich laughter, a thing I had not called to mind for I know not how long.

" I see his coral waistcoat studs that he wore for the first time he dined in my house ; I see his attitude, leaning back a little, already with something of a portly air, and laughing internally. How I admired him ! And now in the West Kirk."

There are many characteristic Stevensonian reflections in the letters written from the Hyères chalet, "that most sweet garden of the universe," in these months of health and activity. Writing of the French and English characters in a letter to Simoneau, with whom Stevenson had boarded at Monterey, he sets them out as follows :

The English	The French
hypocrites	free from hypocrisy
good, stout reliable friends	incapable of friendship
dishonest to the root	fairly honest
fairly decent to women	rather indecent to women.

" There is my table," he wrote, " not at all the usual one, but yes, I think you will agree with it. And by travel, each race can cure much of its defects and acquire much of the others' virtues."

All generalisations about nations are misleading, and in this estimate Stevenson is so conventionally inaccurate that one doubts his powers of observation and independent judgment. The English are no more hypocritical than other peoples. They are shyer than most peoples, and fearful of self-revelation. The French are no more incapable of friendship than the English or the Germans or the Hottentots. There are many honest Frenchmen and many English rogues. The real fundamental difference is that the French are realist and the English romantic. That explains why the English appear decent to women and the French indecent—so far as there is any such appearance—as it explains many other things.

It is at the beginning of their careers that most men are obsessed with the details of craftsmanship, but Stevenson was still constantly concerned with the nature and significance of art and with its relation to life. To Henley he wrote from Hyères : " The essence of art only varies in so far as fashion widens the field of its application ; art is a mill whose thirlage, in different ages, widens and contracts ; but, in any case and under any fashion, the great man produces beauty, terror, and mirth, and the little man produces cleverness (personalities, psychology) instead of beauty, ugliness instead of terror, and jokes instead of mirth. As it was in the beginning, is now and shall be ever, world without end." And to W. H. Low : " In this strange welter where we live, all hangs together by a million filaments ; and to do reasonably well by others, is the first pre-requisite of art. Art is a virtue ; and if I were the man I should be, my art would rise in the proportion of my life."

He was, too, revising some of his own judgments of other writers and becoming more confirmed in his conception of the writer's craft. He said in a letter to his cousin : " Were you to re-read some Balzac, as I have been doing, it would greatly help to clear your eyes. He was a man who never found his method. An inarticulate Shakespeare, smothered under forcible-feeble detail. It is astounding to the riper mind how bad he is, how feeble, how untrue, how tedious ; and, of course, when he surrendered to his temperament, how good and powerful. And yet never plain nor clear. He could not consent to be dull, and thus became so. He would leave nothing undeveloped, and thus drowned out of sight of land amid the multitude of crying and incongruous details. There is but one art—to omit ! O if I knew how to omit, I would ask no other knowledge. A man who knew how to omit would make an *Iliad* of a daily paper."

Christmas 1883 found the Stevensons at the height of their content. Mrs. Stevenson wrote to her mother-in-law :

" What a Christmas of thanksgiving this should be for us all, with Louis so well, his father so well, everything pointing to comfort and happiness. Louis is making such a success with his work, and doing better work every day. Dear mother and father of my beloved husband, I send you Christmas greetings from my heart of hearts. I mean to have a Merry Christmas and be as glad and thankful as possible for all the undeserved mercies and blessings that have been showered upon me." [1]

Mr. Lloyd Osbourne, who went out to Hyères after a year's absence from his mother, says :

" R. L. S. looked very well, and much better than I last remembered him. His hair was cut short ; he wore presentable clothes ; and at a little distance, in a straw hat, he might have been mistaken for an ordinary member of society. The short black cape, or *pèlerine*, that he always preferred to an overcoat was a typically French garment, and in France, of course, aroused no comment. In fact I found that he had become very much of a Frenchman, even to a little ' Imperial ' on his chin. Speaking French as fluently as his

[1] *Life of Mrs. R. L. Stevenson*, by N. V. de G. Sanchez, p. 109.

own language, as familiar with French literature and French politics as with English, nowhere more at home than in his adopted country, he had shed nearly everything English about him." [1]

But the luck was soon to change. Early in the new year Charles Baxter and W. E. Henley came to Hyères and stayed at the chalet for a week, and Stevenson went with them for a short stay in Nice. There he was taken severely ill with congestion of the lungs, and the doctor pronounced that he was dying. And once more the doctor was wrong. Within a month he was able to return to La Solitude. " It was chuck farthing for my life," he said, and though his obstinate courage had ensured a partial recovery, he was never really well again until he had finally left Europe. New complications occurred. Soon after the return to Hyères, he was troubled with ophthalmia, which made it impossible for him to read, and with a bad attack of sciatica. But such was the man, that the greater the affliction, the higher his spirits. In a letter written in March 1884, Mrs. Stevenson says :

" Since he has been unable to read or do anything at all a wonderful change has come over his health, spirits, and temper, all for the better. . . . I wish you could see him with his eye tied up and singing away like mad ; truly like mad, as there is neither time nor method in it, only a large voice." [2]

[1] *Prince Otto*, Introd., p. viii.
[2] *Life of Mrs. R. L. Stevenson*, by N. V. de G. Sanchez, p. 111.

" I may say plainly," he told Henley, " much
as I had lost the power of bearing pain, I had
rather suffer much than die." But the love of
life was sometimes tempered by the necessity of
earning a living : " Whenever I think I would
like to live a little, I hear the butcher's cart re-
sounding through the neighbourhood ; and so to
plunge again. The fault is a good fault for me ;
to be able to do so, is to succeed in life ; and my
life has been a huge success. I can live with joy
and without disgust in the art by which I try to
support myself ; I have the best wife in the world;
I have rather more praise and nearly as much
coin as I deserve ; my friends are many and true-
hearted."

His reading at Hyères was, as usual, extensive
and peculiar. *St. Augustine's Confessions* seemed to
him " Shakespearean in depth." And from St.
Augustine, the sublime, he passed to Barbey
d'Aurevilly, the ridiculous, an " old ass " for
whom he had a sneaking admiration, and then
to Petronius who seemed to him singularly silly.

Perhaps Stevenson had been introduced to the
writings of d'Aurevilly by Edmund Gosse, whose
essay on " the wonderful old fop or beau of the
forties handed down to the eighties in perfect
preservation " is one of the most delightful of
the essays in the volume *French Profiles*. It was
d'Aurevilly's ambition to carry on the work of
Chateaubriand. He was immensely interested in

the ceremonial of the Catholic Church, but in little else. Sir Edmund Gosse says : " He likes the business of a priest, he likes the furniture of a church, but there, in spite of his vehement protestations, his piety seems to a candid reader to have begun and ended." [1] He was a sort of French Disraeli with an immense admiration for dandies and dandyism. He found Dickens vulgar. He was bored both by Goethe and Sainte-Beuve. He was a poseur and a fop who died in a garret with " three melancholy cats the sole mourners by his body." Anatole France wrote that when St. Peter saw Barbey he said :

"Here is M. Barbey d'Aurevilly. He longed to possess all the vices, but failed ; for that is very difficult, and requires a peculiar temperament. He would have liked to wallow in crime, for crime is picturesque ; but he remained the kindliest person in the world, and his life was almost monastic. He has often said bad things, it is true ; but as he never believed them or made anyone else do so, they remained nothing but literature, and his error may be pardoned.

"Chateaubriand, who was also on our side, jeered at us much more seriously during his lifetime." [2]

Why on earth either the man or his writings should have interested Stevenson remains some-

[1] *French Profiles*, by Edmund Gosse, p. 93.
[2] *On Life and Letters*, by Anatole France, Third Series, p. 44.

thing of a mystery. But perhaps I am right, and it was due to Sir Edmund Gosse, for it was Gosse who provided Stevenson with many of his literary idols.

Miss Ferrier, the sister of his dead friend, went out to Hyères early in the spring and stayed there with the Stevensons until they finally left, a fortunate arrangement, since in April Stevenson was again very ill with hemorrhage, weakness, extreme nervousness " that will not let him lie a moment, and damned sciatica o' nights." An outbreak of cholera at Toulon, some three miles away, added to Mrs. Stevenson's anxiety, and in the first week in May, Stevenson had the worst hemorrhage that he had yet suffered. He was choked with blood, and in order to reassure his wife, he scribbled on a piece of paper, " Don't be frightened. If this is death, it is an easy one." But yet once more he pulled round. " In silence in the dark," writes Sir Graham Balfour, " and in acute suffering, he was still cheery and undaunted." " Keep him alive till he is forty," said the doctor, " then although a winged bird, he may land to ninety. But between now and forty he must live the life of an invalid. He must be perfectly tranquil, troubled about nothing, have no shocks or surprises, not even pleasant ones ; must not eat too much, drink too much, laugh too much ; may write a little, but not too much ; talk *very* little and walk no more than

can be helped." [1] He indeed wrote a little even
in these dark weeks, adding new verses to *A Child's
Garden*, writing the best known of his poems, *The
Requiem*, which served as his epitaph in Samoa,
and collaborating with his wife in *The Dynamiter*,
the story suggested by the Fenian outrages in
London. " *The Dynamiter* did double service,"
wrote Mrs. Stevenson, " first as an amusement to
my husband during the tedious hours of his illness, and afterwards as a means of replenishing
our depleted bank account." In the letters
written in the spring of 1884, there is a pretty correspondence with the proof reader of *Young Folk's
Magazine*, who, with great diffidence, pointed out
that in *The Black Arrow* Stevenson had made a
rather important omission. Stevenson wrote him
a cordial letter of thanks :

" I must not, however, allow this opportunity
to go by without once more thanking you—for I
think we have, in a ghostly fashion, met before on
the margin of proof—for the unflagging intelligence and care with which my MS. is read. I
have a large and generally disastrous experience
of printers and printers' readers. Nowhere do I
send worse copy than to *Young Folks*, for with this
sort of story, I rarely re-write ; yet nowhere am I
so well used. And the skill with which the somewhat arbitrary and certainly baffling dialect was
picked up in the case of the *Black Arrow*, filled me

[1] *Life of R. L. Stevenson*, by Graham Balfour, vol. i. p. 215.

with a gentle surprise. I will add that you have humiliated me : that you should have been so much more wide-awake than myself is both humiliating and, I say it very humbly, perhaps flattering." The May hemorrhage meant " a month in bed, a month of silence, a month of not moving without being lifted." Then came a move to Royat, near Clermont-Ferrand, Stevenson still being so ill that he had to be attended by a valet. " We have no money," he wrote to Colvin, " but a valet and a maid. The valet is no end ; how long can you live on a valet ? *Vive le valet.* I am tempted to call myself a valetudinarian."

Mr. Lloyd Osbourne says that it was a mistake that the Stevensons ever left Hyères. But his mother, naturally always anxious, read the *Lancet* and filled her mind with bogeys.

" Vinegar was discovered to be full of perils ; salads carried the eggs of tape-worms ; salt hardened your arteries and shortened your days ; heaven only knows what she discovered in the way of lurking dangers, previously undreamed of ; and when the climax came in an outbreak of cholera in the old part of the town, with a terrible death-roll amongst its poor, dirty, neglected inhabitants, she fell into a panic and began to work on R. L. S. to abandon Hyères as a place too dangerous to live in."

"But for the *Lancet*," says Mr. Lloyd Osbourne, " I doubt if R. L. S. would ever have left Hyères."

The Stevensons returned to London at the end of July, mainly that he should consult Sir Andrew Clark. Stevenson, too, was anxious not to be far away from his father, now obviously near the end of his life, and he and his wife settled at Bournemouth, where the elder Stevenson bought a house as a present for his daughter-in-law. The house was renamed Skerryvore, the name of the best known of the Stevenson lighthouses. They lived at Skerryvore until they left England for good in 1887. Stevenson remained a very sick man all through the three years at Bournemouth. Most of his work was written in bed. For weeks he was not allowed to speak, and he made the rarest excursions from home, one of them being a trip with Henley to Paris, where he met Rodin.

A year later, he paid what was to be his last visit to Paris, with his wife. At the end of a fortnight he announced that he must go home for want of money. Miss Rosaline Masson relates : " Louis had forgotten to cash the father's cheque for £100. And not only had he forgotten to cash it, but he and his wife had supposed themselves to be spending it all that fortnight, whereas they had simply been spending the small supply of ready money they had in hand. Little wonder that they had appeared " visibly disturbed " when they suddenly discovered themselves at the end of their resources.

" It was Thomas Stevenson who, noticing too

large a balance in his bank account, wrote to
Louis about it ; and Louis, after much protest
that the hundred pounds had been spent on the
trip to Paris, found the uncashed cheque among
his own papers, ' beautiful and inviolate,' as Mr.
Low says, ' with all its possibilities. . . .' Alas !
Too late ! That visit might have been extended
to months in sunny France among old scenes, and
with old friends." [1]

His work during these years included the two
plays, *Admiral Guinea* and *Beau Austin*, which he
wrote in collaboration with Henley. He finished
Prince Otto, A Child's Garden of Verses, and *New
Arabian Nights*, and he wrote two of his greatest
successes, *Kidnapped* and *Dr. Jekyll and Mr. Hyde*.

In common with most professional writers,
Stevenson was attracted by the high financial
rewards of the theatre. " The theatre is a gold
mine, and on that I must keep an eye," he wrote
to his father. Henley came down to him at
Bournemouth full of enthusiasm, " a great glowing massive shouldered fellow with a big red
beard and a crutch," as Mr. Lloyd Osbourne has
described him : " jovial, astoundingly clever, and
with a laugh that rolled out like music." [2] He
had come to Bournemouth to make his friends
rich. I again quote Mr. Lloyd Osbourne :
" R. L. S. was no longer to plod along as he had

[1] *The Life of Robert Louis Stevenson*, by Rosaline Masson, p. 243.
[2] *Plays*, Preface, p. vii.

L

been doing ; Henley was to abandon his grinding and ill-paid editorship ; together they would combine to write plays—marvellous plays that would run for hundreds of nights and bring in thousands of pounds ; plays that would revive the perishing drama, now hopelessly given over to imbeciles, who kept yachts and mistresses on money virtually filched from the public ; plays that would be billed on all the hoardings with the electrifying words : ' By Robert Louis Stevenson and William Ernest Henley.' " [1] *Deacon Brodie* had been played at a matinee at the Prince's Theatre on July 2nd with Mr. Henley's brother in the principal part. It was a *succès d'estime*, praised by the critics, but of small interest to the public. Its critical reception, however, was sufficient to justify further experiment. Before the end of the year *Admiral Guinea* and *Beau Austin* were both written, *Beau Austin* in four days, and in the spring of 1885, at Beerbohm Tree's suggestion, they wrote *Macaire*. But the play-writing was not a success, and the fortunes were never earned.

After six years *Beau Austin* was produced at the Haymarket Theatre with a cast that included Beerbohm Tree, Lady Tree, and Fred Terry. Again there was praise from the critics. William Archer declared that the authors had proved that " the aroma of literature can be brought over

[1] *Plays*, Preface, p. ix.

the footlights with stimulating and exhilarating effect." And A. B. Walkley wrote : " Though I checked the players by the book, I never once detected a slip from the elegant idiom of 1820 to the canonised slang of 1890. Indeed, the dialogue throughout was music to the ear and each dress a separate ecstasy for the eye : the whole atmosphere of the play reproduced the subtle aroma of the age of the Dandies." [1] *Macaire* was produced by the Stage Society in 1900, and was afterwards acted once or twice by Beerbohm Tree and Weedon Grossmith. *Admiral Guinea* was produced at His Majesty's Theatre in 1909, when Elizabeth Robins spoke the Prologue.

Macaire was published by Henley in the *New Review* in June 1895. Bernard Shaw described it as a " famous writer of fiction collaborating with a born master of verse to rescue a famous old harlequinade from obsolescence." " The charm of the pair," he said, " was their combination of artistic faculty with a pleasant boyishness of imagination." [2]   And Henley was dismissed with the curt remark, " He has imagination without sense."

In his study of Henley, Mr. Kennedy Williamson has quoted Mr. Granville Barker's judgment of the plays :

" I have a qualified admiration for the plays,

[1] *Playhouse Impressions*, by A. B. Walkley, p. 109.
[2] *Dramatic Opinions*, by G. B. Shaw, vol. i. pp. 124 and 128.

but H. and S. never quite got away (I think) from their ' toy theatre ' days—they thought the theatre great fun as a plaything.   They had *literary* conscience—and that appears in all the writing.   But as to the main essential part of the business, I don't believe they ever felt the necessity of losing themselves in that, as they were ready to in a poem or a novel.   Hence there is a surface effect of a sort gained, and how much that can be made to count for, well, only experiment can show.   But the things ring rather hollow.   *Deacon Brodie* was, I believe, merely put together to give Henley's brother, the actor, an effective part.   *Beau Austin* and *Admiral Guinea* are the two best, and the latter the better of them in my judgment.   *Macaire* is a disciplining into decent shape of the hotch-potch that Lemaître gave life to and that other (English) actors followed him in.   But it remains a skeleton that has to be clothed with flesh ; and I 'm not very sure they understood that." [1]

The truth was, that Stevenson knew nothing of the theatre—when he started play-writing, he had not seen a play for years—and Henley knew nothing of stagecraft.   Stevenson, indeed, soon began to regret what he realised must be an unproductive waste of time.   His illness was a constant heavy expense.   It was impossible for him to live cheaply.   He remained to a considerable extent dependent on his father.   He must do the work

[1] *W. E. Henley*, by Kennedy Williamson, p. 104.

that he knew that he could do, and for which he now had a market, and he was a sufficiently good critic of his own writing to know that the plays were not good. " The reperusal of the *Admiral* was a sore blow," he wrote to Henley, " eh, God, man, it is a low, black, dirty, blackguard, ragged piece : vomitable in many parts—simply vomitable." *Macaire* seemed to him " a piece of jobwork, hurriedly bockled ; might have been worse, might have been better ; happy-go-lucky ; act it or-let-it-rot piece of business." And again he wrote to Henley : " I have thought as well as I could of what you said ; and I come unhesitatingly to the opinion that the stage is only a lottery, must not be regarded as a trade, and must never be preferred to drudgery. If money comes from any play, let us regard it as a legacy, but never count upon it in our income for the year." So the theatre dream was abandoned. Stevenson's only other essay in play-writing was in collaboration with his wife in a play called *The Hanging Judge*, which has never been acted.

The failure of the plays was the beginning of the estrangement between Stevenson and Henley. Nearly all Stevenson's friends became his wife's friends, but not Henley. He was a stronger man than Stevenson. For a while he dominated him, but the domination came to an end with Stevenson's marriage, and Henley, the he-man before Hollywood was invented, scorned him as wife-ridden.

Mr. Kennedy Williamson quotes Sir Sidney Colvin.
I have no other record of the note :

" For all his crippled condition, Henley was in talk the most boisterously untiring, the lustiest and most stimulating of companions, and could never bring himself to observe the consideration due to Louis' frail health and impaired lungs. . . . Anxiety on this account was the main cause of the wife's disliking his society for her husband. . . . No doubt also the practical failure of the experiment in play-writing on which Stevenson spent so much effort with little or no result, in conjunction with this same friend, made the wife regard the friendship as one which brought a dangerous amount of exertion with no corresponding advantages." [1]

Kidnapped was the only productive result of Stevenson's brief enthusiasm for the theatre. In order to obtain material for *The Hanging Judge*, the Stevensons commissioned a London bookseller to send them the reports of Old Bailey trials. Occasionally the reports of other trials were contained in the parcel, and among them was the trial of James Stewart for the murder of Colin Campbell of Glenure. From this report Stevenson derived his first idea of the character of Alan Breck, perhaps his happiest creation, as Walter Raleigh described him, " one of the most lovable characters in all fiction."

[1] *W. E. Henley*, by Kennedy Williamson, p. 260.

Treasure Island had given Stevenson a fiction public, and with *Prince Otto* he endeavoured to exploit that public with a far more ambitious and more subtle achievement. *Prince Otto* is essentially a study of character, fantastic and artificial, but true to the observation and experience of its author. Mrs. Stevenson says that the character of Prince Otto was originally modelled on Stevenson's cousin, but it came more and more to resemble the man Stevenson believed himself to be, but which his wife knew he was not. " Otto shirked responsibility, my husband courted it. Gondremark could never have laid his hands on the reins of government in Grünewald had Robert Louis Stevenson been the reigning prince. Otto, the gentle philosopher, preferred a life of peace and comfortable domesticity. My husband, on the contrary, was of a bolder spirit and looked upon peace and comfort as stumbling blocks for the soul." [1] But perhaps Stevenson knew himself better than his wife knew him. Happily love wears rose-coloured spectacles. Perhaps the revolt against peace and comfortable domesticity was merely the revolt of the sick man who, for his soul's sake, had to pretend to a life of strife and adventure from which he was, as a matter of fact, entirely shut away.

Although *Prince Otto* earned the praise of George Meredith, it was not on the whole well received.

[1] *Prince Otto*, Preface, p. xiii.

Stevenson wrote to Gosse : " The *Prince* has done fairly well in spite of the reviews, which have been bad ; he was, as you doubtless saw, well slated in the *Saturday* ; one paper received it as a child's story ; another (picture my agony) described it as a ' Gilbert comedy.' "

He was seriously disappointed. The book had been difficult to write. Its fantasy demanded a certain artificiality of line, and his wife has described it as "the last effort of his earlier manner." He said to Gosse : " You aim high and you take longer over your work and it will not be so successful as if you had aimed low and rushed it." It had been an infinitely more difficult task to write *Prince Otto* than to write *Treasure Island*, but who will now say that *Prince Otto* is comparable to *Treasure Island* as a work of literary art ? The truth, of course, is that the ultimate value of an achievement has very little to do with the labour with which it has been achieved, and whatever else genius may or may not be, it is certainly not an infinite capacity for taking pains.

Kidnapped was more or less deliberately a return to the *Treasure Island* manner. Stevenson thought it a " far better story and far sounder at heart." He wrote to Watts-Dunton : " I began it partly as a lark, partly as a pot-boiler ; and suddenly it moved, David and Alan stepped out from the canvas, and I found I was in another world. But there was the cursed beginning, and a cursed end must be appended ; and our old friend Byles the butcher was plainly audible tapping at the back door. So it had to go into the world, one part (as it does seem to me) alive, one part merely galvanised : no work, only an essay." It would seem that Stevenson thought a good deal better of *Kidnapped* than some of his letters would suggest, and it was highly praised by the critics, whose opinions he valued most. Before the story was finished, he had decided to leave the door open for a sequel since, as he told his father, " Colvin thinks it sin and folly to throw away David and Alan Breck upon so small a field as this one."

Kidnapped has many scenes of great dramatic force, and it is written with those gleaming sentences which never failed its author. It was the first of Stevenson's Scottish stories, and as a novel it is the obvious inferior of *Catriona*, its sequel. In it, as in all its successors, Stevenson shows himself, as Mr. Chesterton has said, as " being intellectually on the side of the Whigs and morally on the side of the Jacobites." The artist in him was inevitably with Bonnie Prince Charlie, the Shorter Catechist was with the Covenanters.

In his essay, *A Chapter on Dreams*, written long before the theorising of Freud and Jung, Stevenson wrote :

" When the bank begins to send letters and the butcher to linger at the back gate, he sets to belabouring his brains after a story, for that is the readiest money-winner ; and, behold ! at once the little people begin to bestir themselves in the same quest, and labour all night long, and all night long set before him truncheons of tales upon their lighted theatre. No fear of his being frightened now ; the flying heart and the frozen scalp are things bygone ; applause, growing applause, growing interest, growing exultation in his own cleverness (for he takes all the credit), and at last a jubilant leap to wakefulness, with the cry, ' I have it, that 'll do ! ' upon his lips ; with such and similar emotions he sits at these nocturnal dramas, with such outbreaks, like Claudius in the play, he scatters the performance in the midst. Often enough the waking is a disappointment ; he has been too deep asleep, as I explain the thing ; drowsiness has gained his little people, they have gone stumbling and maundering through their parts ; and the play, to the awakened mind, is seen to be a tissue of absurdities. And yet how often have these sleepless Brownies done him honest service, and given him, as he sat idly taking his pleasure in the boxes, better tales than he could fashion for himself."

So far as his biographers know, the sleepless Brownies only provided him with the plots for two of his stories, for *Olalla* and for *The Strange Case of Dr. Jekyll and Mr. Hyde*. One night, Mrs. Stevenson was awakened by her husband screaming with horror. She woke him and he explained:

" I was dreaming a fine bogey tale," and the next morning he started to write *Dr. Jekyll and Mr. Hyde*, finishing, so she said, thirty thousand words in three days, and the whole book in a week ; a marvellous piece of industry for a sick man. Mrs. Stevenson was critical. She felt he had missed the point and had allowed himself to be lured into sensationalism, and Mr. Lloyd Osbourne relates that for once there was a hectic scene between his mother and his stepfather. Stevenson was at last convinced that his wife was right, and to her discomfiture he threw the whole MS. at the back of the fire and started to write it again. Mr. Lloyd Osbourne writes :

" Then ensued another three days' feverish industry on his part, and of a hushed, anxious and tiptoeing anticipation on ours ; of meals where he scarcely spoke ; of evenings unenlivened by his presence ; of awed glimpses of him, sitting up in bed, writing, writing, writing, with the counterpane littered with his sheets. The culmination was the *Jekyll and Hyde* that every one knows ; that, translated into every European tongue and many Oriental, has given a new phrase to the world.

" The writing of it was an astounding feat, from whatever aspect it may be regarded. Sixty-four thousand words in six days ; more than ten thousand words a day. To those who know little of such things I may explain that a thousand

words a day is a fair average for any writer of
fiction. Anthony Trollope set himself this quota ;
it was Jack London's ; it is—and has been—a
sort of standard of daily literary accomplishment.
Stevenson multiplied it by ten ; and on top of
that copied out the whole in another two days,
and had it in the post on the third !

" It was a stupendous achievement ; and the
strange thing was that instead of showing lassitude afterwards, he seemed positively refreshed
and revitalised : went about with a happy air ;
was as uplifted as though he had come into a
fortune ; looked better than he had for months." ¹

Forty thousand copies of the English edition of
Dr. Jekyll and Mr. Hyde were sold in six months.
The book was widely pirated in America ; plays
were founded on it ; it was quoted by preachers,
and made the subject of leading newspaper
articles ; and even Symonds, who hated everything popular, and was always Stevenson's most
severe critic, admitted that " the art is burning
and intense."   The theme of a dual personality is
almost as old as human thought.   But Stevenson
gave it a new significance.   It is impossible to
better Mr. Chesterton's summary : " The real
stab of the story is not in the discovery that the
one man is two men, but in the discovery that the
two men are one man "—the evil and good war-
ring with each other, with the moral, and an

¹ *Jekyll and Hyde*, Preface, p. xi.

awful moral it is—and I turn back to Mr. Chesterton—that while Jekyll created Hyde, Hyde destroyed Jekyll.

Stevenson was a writer of recognised and established position long before the publication of *Dr.
Jekyll and Mr. Hyde*. Publishers were eager to
produce his books, and so long as he could write,
he was assured a moderate income. But *Jekyll
and Hyde* made him famous, even more famous in
America than in England, and when the Bournemouth period came to an end in 1887, his struggle
with penury had definitely come to an end.

Something must be said of the friendships of
the Bournemouth years. To the circle of his old
Savile Club friends were added many others : John
Sargent, who painted a rather fantastic portrait of
him of which Mrs. Stevenson strongly disap-
proved, William Archer, the well-known dramatic
critic and a brother Scot, and Henry James.
Mrs. Stevenson wrote to her mother-in-law :

" We have a very pleasant visitor. One evening a card was handed in with ' Henry James '
upon it. He spent that evening, asked to come
again the next night, arriving almost before we
had got done with dinner, and staying as late as
he thought he might, and asking to come the next
evening, which is to-night. I call that very flattering. I had always been told that he was the
type of an Englishman, but except that he looks
like the Prince of Wales, I call him the type

of an American. He is gentle, amiable, and soothing." [1]

Stevenson continually corresponded with Henry James, and the friendship was an invaluable asset to the Bournemouth years. They often disagreed. They had a published argument on the function of the novel. Stevenson, "a sincere admirer," deplored the fact that James's characters were not conceived "in a mould a little more abstract and academic," and that his incidents were not related "in a slightly more emphatic key." But who can conceive an emphatic Henry James?

It was while he was living at Bournemouth that the picturesque legend of Stevenson, the sick man in a smoking-cap, first became popular. He was now a celebrity, the prey of the photographer, and many portraits, still familiar, date back to Bournemouth. Mrs. Stevenson says :

" The English climate is treacherous, and even in Bournemouth we had to exercise the utmost caution in guarding the invalid from draughts and cold. The doctor would not allow my husband even to have his hair cut unless both the state of his health and the weather were propitious. The photographs mark these changes like a barometer. A likeness with long hair meant a severe illness ; all those taken in Samoa, where he enjoyed the best health of his life, show him with his hair cut short." [2]

[1] *Life of Mrs. R. L. Stevenson*, by N. V. de G. Sanchez, p. 122.
[2] *Prince Otto*, Preface, p. xv.

Stevenson was no mere literary recluse. He
was keenly and, in his inevitable manner, often
tumultuously interested in public affairs. He
violently denounced Gladstone and all his ways.
After the Gordon tragedy, he felt that England
was degraded, and that he himself was degraded,
and he declared that if he were to write to Gladstone he would sign himself "your fellow criminal
in the eyes of God." The nation was degraded
because it believed in nothing, and harking back
to his Paris days, he saw in the degradation the
victory of the hated bourgeoisie. " *Voilà le bourgeois, le voilà nu,*" he wrote in a letter to Symonds.
His indignation at the Land League outrages in
Ireland was equally hectic. Mr. Chesterton has
pointed out that while Stevenson lacked nothing
of sympathy with the Scottish crofters, he had
none at all for the rack-rented Irish peasants. He
seriously proposed a particularly fantastic method
of showing his sympathy for the victims of the
Land League agitation. In November 1885,
John Curtin was murdered by a party of Moon-
lighters, and his family were afterwards the victims of an extremely thorough boycott. To
Stevenson, the family were the victims of English
cowardice, and he suggested that he and his
family should go to Ireland, take over the Curtin
farm and, if necessary, be murdered. " The
murder of a distinguished English literary man
and his family, thus engaged in the assertion of

human rights, will arrest the horror of the whole civilised world, and bring down its odium on these miscreants." [1]

Mr. Lloyd Osbourne ascribes this quixotic plan to the influence of Tolstoy. He had been considerably disturbed on coming down from Edinburgh University, where he was then a student, to discover that Stevenson had " got religion." But Stevenson always had religion, Scottish not Russian, though he certainly read a good deal of Russian literature at Bournemouth—Dostoevsky perhaps more than Tolstoy. Mr. Lloyd Osbourne says :

" Tolstoy had a profound influence over him and did much to formulate his vague and sometimes contradictory views. Tolstoy virtually rediscovered Christianity as a stupendous force in the world ; not the Christianity of dogma, supernaturalism, hell, and heaven, but as a sublime ethical formula that alone could redeem society. Stevenson in this sense was an ardent Christian. It was characteristic of him to say : ' Christ was always such a great gentleman ; you can always count on His doing the right thing,' and he used to instance, the marriage-feast at Cana with a special pleasure. ' What a charming courtesy to these poor people—to help their entertainment with a better wine ! ' " [2]

[1] *Jekyll and Hyde*, Preface, p. xiii.
[2] *New Arabian Nights*, Introd., p. xvi.

But Stevenson's ambition to be murdered in Ireland, about which and its people he knew nothing, had little to do with Tolstoy. It was just one more example of the perfectly sincere play-acting which was an essential, perhaps the most essential, part of his character. Sir Sidney Colvin says that Stevenson was never quite satisfied that he had done right in giving way to the persuasion and protest of his wife and stepson not to go to Ireland, but the project was definitely brought to an end by the death of his father.

Few men, certainly no man of letters, has ever owed more to his father than Robert Louis owed to Thomas Stevenson, and nothing in the history of literature is more grotesque than the pretence that Thomas Stevenson was the typical Philistine unable to appreciate the genius of his son. He was often bewildered, often saddened, but he was never lacking in generosity, and in later years he certainly was never lacking in admiration and understanding. Despite the pose of poverty, Stevenson responded to the fullest degree. In earlier years he had always understood the depth of his father's character, and he was never ungrateful for his generosity. After his father's death, he wrote of him :

" He was a man of somewhat antique strain : with a blended sternness and softness that was wholly Scottish and at first somewhat bewildering ; with a profound essential melancholy of

M

disposition and (what often accompanies it) the most humorous geniality in company ; shrewd and childish ; passionately attached, passionately prejudiced ; a man of many extremes, many faults of temper, and no very stable foothold for himself among life's troubles. . . . For all these emotional extremes, and in spite of the melancholy ground of his character, he had upon the whole a happy life ; nor was he less fortunate in his death, which at last came to him unaware."

And there is sincerity of admiration and affection in the poem :

TO MY FATHER

In the first hour, the seaman in his skiff
Moves through the unmoving bay, to where the town
Its earliest smoke into the air upbreathes,
And the rough hazels climb along the beach.

To the tugg'd oar the distant echo speaks.
The ship lies resting, where by reef and roost
Thou and thy lights have led her like a child.

This hast thou done, and I—can I be base ?
I must arise, O father, and to port
Some lost, complaining seaman pilot home.

Mr. Lloyd Osbourne says that Stevenson never really liked Bournemouth. " The Victorianism it exemplified was jarring to every feeling he possessed." He was always ill there. He had only remained in England knowing that his father's life could not continue for very long, and because he was properly anxious to be near him at the time of his death.

Henry James once said that Mrs. Stevenson was " the exploiter of climates," but when, after his father's death, the doctors urged the necessity of Stevenson leaving England, it was she and not he who lamented the move. "Life had been too happy at Skerryvore. The envying gods had struck it down." Stevenson, on the other hand, was delighted at the idea of going back to America. He hated remaining for long in one place and rejoiced once again to be on the move. On August 21st, 1887, with his mother, his wife, and his stepson, he sailed for the second time for New York.

CHAPTER IX

THE LAST EXILE

STEVENSON was brought from Bournemouth
to London miserably ill. He stayed for a
night at a private hotel in Finsbury Circus, where
he was visited by Edmund Gosse and others of his
friends. Sir Edmund Gosse has recorded : " His
position was one which might have daunted any
man's spirit, doomed to exile, in miserable health,
starting vaguely across the Atlantic, with all his
domestic interests rooted up, and with no notion
where, or if at all, they should be replanted. If
ever a man of imagination could be excused for
repining, it was now. But Louis showed no
white feather. He was radiantly humorous and
romantic." [1]

The only new book that he wanted to take with
him was Thomas Hardy's *The Woodlanders*. Both
Edmund Gosse and Sidney Colvin somehow contrived to secure him the three volumes on a Sunday afternoon, a striking example of persistent
friendship. Among the other parting presents
that he received was a case of champagne from
Henry James, to which he referred gratefully in
the letters written during the voyage.

[1] *Critical Kit-Kats*, by Edmund Gosse, p. 297.

The Stevensons sailed to America in a cattle ship called the *Ludgate Hill*, which took in a cargo of horses, monkeys, and other strange beasts at Havre. It would seem due to his habitual freakishness that he had selected so uncomfortable a vessel, for he had inherited from his father some three thousand pounds, the larger part of which he afterwards spent in chartering a yacht for his first voyage on the Pacific. But Stevenson enjoyed, or at least professed to enjoy the voyage. " It was lovely on our stable-ship chock full of stallions," he wrote to Sidney Colvin. " She rolled heartily, rolled some of the fittings out of our state-room, and I think a more dangerous cruise (except that it was summer) would be hard to imagine. But we enjoyed it to the mast-head, all but Fanny ; and even she perhaps a little." Mrs. Stevenson's lot was certainly no easy one ! Stevenson wrote of her :

> Here from the sea the unfruitful sun shall rise,
> Bathe the bare deck and blind the unshielded eyes ;
> The allotted hours aloft shall wheel in vain
> And in the unpregnant ocean plunge again.
> Assault of squalls that mock the watchful guard,
> And pluck the bursting canvas from the yard,
> And senseless clamour of the calm, at night
> Must mar your slumbers. By the plunging light,
> In beetle-haunted, most unwomanly bower
> Of the wild-swerving cabin, hour by hour . . .

In a letter to Henry James he said : " I caught cold on the Banks, after having had the finest time conceivable, and enjoyed myself more than I could have hoped on board our strange floating menagerie ; stallions and monkeys and matches made our cargo ; and the vast continent of these incongruities rolled the while like a haystack ; and the stallions stood hypnotised by the motion, looking through the ports at our dinner-table, and winked when the crockery was broken ; and the little monkeys stared at each other in their cages, and were thrown overboard like little bluish babies." No wonder when they eventually arrived in New York, he should record : " My wife is a good deal run down, and I am no great shakes."

Stevenson landed in New York to find himself famous. Before he left London, he had been elected to the Athenæum Club under the rule that secures election for distinguished men of letters. But in America there was for him a greater glory. Sir Graham Balfour relates that when the pilot came on board the *Ludgate Hill*, it turned out that he was known on his boat as Hyde, while his better-tempered partner was called Jekyll.[1] Stevenson was pursued by a host of newspaper interviewers. " It is very silly and not pleasant except where humour enters," he told Colvin, " and I confess the poor interviewer lads pleased me. They are too good for their trade ; avoided anything I asked them to avoid, and were no

[1] *Life of R. L. Stevenson*, by Graham Balfour, vol. ii. p. 26.

more vulgar in their reports than they could
help."

He was at once offered highly remunerative
work. The *New York World* suggested paying
him two thousand pounds a year for an article a
week. But this he refused. He contracted with
Scribner's to write them twelve articles for seven
hundred pounds, and he was offered sixteen hundred pounds for the serial rights of his next story.
" I hold," he said, " that £700 a year is as much
as anybody can possibly want ; and I have had
more, so I know, for the extry coins were for no
use, excepting for illness, which damns everything."

It had been intended that Stevenson should
settle for a time in Colorado Springs, six thousand
feet above the sea. But this high altitude was
impossible for his wife, and it was decided that
they should stay some months in the Adirondack
Mountains on the shores of Saranac Lake, and
there they arrived on October 3rd, 1887, and
stayed until the spring of the next year. The
place was lonely and the climate seems to have
been abominable, but thanks, possibly, to the
help of a first-rate physician, Stevenson's health
definitely improved during the winter. In January, the temperature was thirty degrees below
zero, and the cost of living was very high. " Saranac is not quite so dear in some ways as the rest
of this land," he wrote to Henley, " where it costs

you a pound to sneeze and fifty to blow your nose." Among the presents that he received from England was a copy of Gleeson White's delightful collection of Ballades and Rondeaux, long since, unhappily, out of print, and one is inclined to doubt Stevenson's critical faculty when one discovers that he described it as "a ridiculous volume."

In the "harsh, crude, doleful climate" of Saranac, which, by the way, the sturdy Scottish Mrs. Stevenson the elder seems to have enjoyed, Stevenson was feverishly busy. His main preoccupation was with the essays that he had contracted to write for Scribner's. One of the best of them, *The Lantern Bearers*, is a restatement of his philosophy in which, as always, the Hedonist struggles with the Shorter Catechist. He is concerned with "the crown of a man's joy," and he once again tilts against realistic fiction, greatly daring to write a sweeping condemnation of Tolstoy's *Powers of Darkness*, of which he wrote : "A work which dwells on the ugliness of crime and gives no hint of any loveliness in the temptation, sins against the modesty of life, and even when a Tolstoy writes it, sinks to melodrama."

In addition to the essays, Stevenson largely rewrote Lloyd Osbourne's *The Wrong Box*, and began *The Master of Ballantrae*, the last chapters of which were written months later in Honolulu. Surely no other novel has ever been begun in a

bleak temperature well under zero, and finished
in the balmy air of the Pacific Islands. The
theme of *The Master of Ballantrae* had been long in
his mind. Mrs. Stevenson says that the early
part of the story was conceived while he was staying at Braemar in 1881. But he himself has related that it had been thought out " on the moors
between Pitlochry and Strathairdle, conceived in
Highland rain in the blend of the smell of heather
and bog plants." [1] Certainly the smell of the
heather is instinct in *The Master of Ballantrae*,
though it was written by a Scotsman in exile.

Another task of this winter was the revising of
The Black Arrow, of which Mrs. Stevenson thought
very little. It may, indeed, not unfairly be regarded as the only pot-boiler that her husband
ever wrote. Just because Mrs. Stevenson dis-
approved, the book was dedicated to her, and in
the dedication her husband wrote : " I have
watched with interest, with pain, and at length
with amusement, your unavailing attempts to
peruse the *Black Arrow* ; I think I should lack
humour indeed if I let the occasion slip and did
not place your name in the fly-leaf of the only
book of mine that you have never read—and never
will read." [2]

Music was one of Stevenson's diversions during his illnesses, and at Saranac he wrote sets of

[1] *Life of R. L. Stevenson*, by Graham Balfour, vol. ii. p. 31.
[2] *Life of Mrs. R. L. Stevenson*, by N. V. de G. Sanchez, p. 130.

words to Beethoven's *Variations Faciles*. He continued to read prodigiously, interspersing the steady perusal of the *Æneid* with the new books sent him by his friends in England. Among them was Mr. Bernard Shaw's first novel, *Cashel Byron's Profession*, of which he wrote :

" MY DEAR ARCHER,—What am I to say? I have read your friend's book with singular relish. If he has written any other, I beg you will let me see it ; and if he has not, I beg him to lose no time in supplying the deficiency. It is full of promise ; but I should like to know his age. There are things in it that are very clever, to which I attach small importance ; it is the shape of the age. And there are passages, particularly the rally in presence of the Zulu king, that show genuine and remarkable narrative talent—a talent that few will have the wit to understand, a talent of strength, spirit, capacity, sufficient vision, and sufficient self-sacrifice, which last is the chief point in a narrator.

" As a whole, it is (of course) a fever dream of the most feverish. Over Bashville the footman I howled with derision and delight ; I dote on Bashville—I could read of him for ever ; *de Bashville je suis le fervent*—there is only one Bashville, and I am his devoted slave ; *Bashville est magnifique, mais il n'est guère possible.* He is the note of the book. It is all mad, mad and deliriously delightful ; the author has a taste in chivalry like

Walter Scott's or Dumas', and then he daubs in
little bits of socialism ; he soars away on the wings
of the romantic griffon—even the griffon, as he
cleaves air, shouting with laughter at the nature
of the quest—and I believe in his heart he thinks
he is labouring in a quarry of solid granite realism.

"It is this that makes me—the most hardened
adviser now extant—stand back and hold my
peace. If Mr. Shaw is below five-and-twenty, let
him go his path ; if he is thirty, he had best be
told that he is a romantic, and pursue romance
with his eyes open ;—or perhaps, he knows it ;—
God knows !—my brain is softened.

"It is HORRID FUN. All I ask is more of it.
Thank you for the pleasure you gave us, and tell
me more of the inimitable author.

"(say, Archer, my God, what women !).—
Yours very truly,
"ROBERT LOUIS STEVENSON."

"1 part Charles Reade ; 1 part Henry James
or some kindred author badly assimilated ; ½ part
Disraeli (perhaps unconscious) ; 1½ parts strugg-
ling, over-laid original talent ; 1 part blooming,
gaseous folly. That is the equation as it stands ;
what it may be, I don't know, nor any other man.
Vixere fortes—O, let him remember that—let him
beware of his damned century ; his gifts of insane chivalry and animated narration are just
those that might be slain and thrown out like an

untimely birth by the Daemon of the epoch. And if he only knew how I have adored the chivalry! *Bashville!—O Bashville! j'en chortle* (which is fairly polyglot."   R. L. S.

Has anything better been since written of Mr. Shaw? "Horrid fun" is certainly an accurate description of one act of *The Apple Cart.* The criticism, too, "My God, what women!" might be applied with equal justice to all Mr. Shaw's later writings, in which all the women are as unnatural as Dickens's Agnes, except when they are Mr. Bernard Shaw.

In a letter to Henry James there is an acute reference to Meredith, for whose genius he had the most profound admiration. He says: "I was vexed at your account of my admired Meredith; I wish I could go and see him; as it is I will try to write; and yet (do you understand me?) there is something in that potent, *genialisch* affectation that puts one on the strain even to address him in a letter. He is not an easy man to be yourself with; there is so much of him, and the veracity and the high athletic intellectual humbug are so intermixed."

Of his own literary projects, *The Master of Ballantrae,* one of the greatest of his achievements, was most in his mind. "No thought have I now apart from it," he wrote to Colvin. "It is to me a most seizing tale; there are some fantastic elements ; the most is a dead genuine human problem—human tragedy, I should say rather." " Five parts of it are bound, human tragedy," he told Henry James. " The last one or two I regret to say not so soundly designed ; I almost hesitate to write them; they are very picturesque, but they are fantastic ; they shame, perhaps degrade the beginning." The design seemed to him daring, and as he planned it, it was to be the longest book that he had yet written.

While he was working on the gloomy shore of the Saranac Lake, Stevenson was constantly dreaming of the sunshine and the sea. The sea was in his blood. Was he not the descendant of a famous family of lighthouse builders ? Everything to do with ships and boats had always interested him, and he had hotly defended himself against Henley's charge that he was ignorant of technical nautical details. During these winter evenings he was planning a long, lazy voyage on a chartered yacht to the islands of the Pacific, the expense of which was to be met by syndicated essays in the American Press, and he and young Lloyd Osbourne discussed the islands and the sunshine " as the snow drove against our frozen windows ; as the Arctic day closed in, gloomy and wild, and snow-shoes and buffalo-coats were put by to steam in corners while we gathered round the lamp."

In the spring of 1888, Mrs. Stevenson went to

San Francisco with the idea of chartering the yacht. Stevenson stayed for a while in New York, where he met Mark Twain, and then settled for a month in New Jersey. It was while he was living here that the break occurred with Henley, to which there is no reference in the authorised biography, and which Sir Sidney Colvin describes as " a quarrel in defence of his wife which had been fastened on him by one of his oldest friends and was never afterwards fully healed." The break hurt Stevenson very deeply : " When I am alone," he wrote to his wife, " I think of nothing but the one affair. Say nothing of it to anyone, please. If things go to the worst, we must bear this in mere silence." [1]

Henley and Stevenson were bound together by the same heroic struggle with ill-health and the same love of words. But in fundamentals no two men were ever more unlike. Henley has been brilliantly described by Mr. Robert Lynd as " Pistol with a style." He was vain-glorious, over-vehement, impatient, always in revolt against God and man. Life had treated him badly, and he shouted back at life and challenged it to do its worst. He was " the crippled but undefeated lion," roaring not to keep his courage up, for that was never necessary, but for the sheer joy of defiance. He was immensely boastful, and not without reason. His soul was unconquerable, and

[1] *The Master of Ballantrae*, Introd., p. xii.

he was the captain of it, though neither he nor any other man has ever been master of his fate.

Henley was a pagan, an embittered and, for all his courage, a pathetically hopeless pagan. Mr. Chesterton complains that Henley had lost "the natural reaction of a man against a tyrant." But Henley could never have lost a reaction that he was incapable of experiencing. He and Charles Whibley and the smaller men whom they influenced really believed that the one hope for the human race was that it should be guided by the heavy hand of a tyrant, and it was a matter of quite secondary importance to them whether the tyrant were benevolent or not.

But with it all, Henley was a brave man and, in many respects, a great man. Neither in his virtues nor in his failings was he the least like Stevenson. For Henley, writes Mr. Lynd, "most seas were Dead Seas and most shores were desolate."[1] For Stevenson all seas were enchanted seas and all shores were the shores of fairyland. Henley was a realist. For him, as Mr. Chesterton has said of another writer, "everything pretty must be pretence." To Stevenson all pretence was pretty. And he loved prettily to pretend as in the verse :

> Wealth I ask not, hope nor love,
> Nor a friend to know me ;
> All I ask, the heaven above
> And the road below me.

---

[1] *Books and Authors*, by Robert Lynd, p. 201.

Stevenson was something more than a romanti-
cist, he was a fantastic. Henley could never have
dressed up, he could never make-believe. But
Stevenson was always dressing up, and he lived
his days in the land of make-believe.

Henley made many enemies, but he spent himself in the service of his friends. George Wynd-
ham eulogised his exuberant generosity. Mr.
Cope Cornford has paid tribute to his loyalty and
kindness. He certainly gave far more than he
ever received.

Stevenson had many friends who delighted to
serve him. He attracted affection by his charm,
but he bought affection very cheaply, generally
repaying tiresome service with a sermon or a
sonnet, both of which came very easy to him.
His letters amply justify Mr. Benson in writing :
" He was content to use their invaluable services
to him and to inhale the abundant incense, re-
warding them with delightful prattle about himself, but scarcely ever do we find a sign that he
misses or needs them. He was too busy with his
work to respond to the demands of intimacy ; he
was one of those very attractive people who inspire rather than render friendship. . . . His
power of attraction was infinitely stronger than
his power of affection, he reaped a great deal
where he had not sown much." [1] No one gave
him so much as his wife, and there is an oddly

[1] *London Mercury*, July 1925, pp. 279, 281.

illuminating sentence in *Catriona* : " It always warms a man to see a woman brave."

Mr. Lloyd Osbourne has said : " Although R. L. S. always wrote so feelingly about his friends, it was remarkable how well he could do without them. Few men had so little need of intimacies as he. Human intercourse of some kind was essential ; it was the breath of life to him ; but anyone with any originality of mind and power of expression would suffice." [1]

Henley was always poor and often hard put to it to pay his bills. Stevenson was never really poor, for in emergencies his father's purse never failed him. It pleased him to pretend to abject poverty, but that was part of the game of make-believe. " We all suffer ourselves to be too much concerned about a little poverty," Stevenson wrote sententiously. But he suffered himself to be concerned by a purely imaginary poverty ! Despite his very poverty, Mr. Cornford says that Henley " never considered either gain or the public for a moment." On the other hand, his letters show how constantly gain and the public were in Stevenson's mind, and it seems probable that if he had thought of neither he might never have written fiction, except to amuse Mr. Lloyd Osbourne.

Henley was the greater man, Stevenson in-finitely the more human and lovable. Their

[1] *Prince Otto*, Introd., p. ix.

N

friendship could not in the nature of things have endured for ever. It is remarkable that it lasted so long. To Henley, Stevenson's moralisings and posings (an intrinsic part of him though they were) were intolerable. To Stevenson, Henley's criticisms were equally intolerable, for Stevenson asked nothing from his friends but praise. He hated criticism, and Henley never spared his intimates. Stevenson wrote in one of his poems :

> O Henley, in my hours of ease
> You may say anything you please,
> But when I join the Muse's revel,
> Begad, I wish you at the devil !

In nothing were the two men more different than in their attitude to death. Henley may have suffered more actual pain than Stevenson, but he was not so persistently threatened by death. Still, the thought of it was constantly with him, and generally to him its coming was to be welcomed.

> For the end I know is the best of all.

And death must be jeered at as life must be jeered at, with the similes of the town that Henley affected :

> Madam Life 's a piece in bloom,
>   Death goes dogging everywhere ;
> She 's the tenant of the room,
>   He 's the ruffian on the stair.

You shall see her as a friend,
You shall bilk him once and twice ;
But he 'll trap you in the end,
And he 'll stick you for her price.

Compare the poem with the following from
Stevenson's *Will o' the Mill* :

" You are a strange physician," said Will, looking
steadfastly upon his guest.
" I am a natural law," he replied, " and people call
me Death."
" Why did you not tell me so at first ? " cried Will.
" I have been waiting for you these many years.   Give
me your hand, and welcome."

Henley lived hardly.   Stevenson lived gladly.
He could not forget death.   He was not afraid,
but he most assuredly hated the idea of dying.
For Stevenson life was (I think this is exactly true)
a twopence coloured adventure.   To Henley it
was rather a sorry business :

Struggle and turmoil, revel and brawl—
Youth is the sign of them, one and all.
A smouldering hearth and a silent stage—
These are a type of the world of Age.

Henley was a stubborn sick Englishman, ever
in courageous and bitter rebellion against the
bludgeoning of fate, while Stevenson was a sick
Covenanter who contrived to enjoy bad health.
" I am pretty happy on the whole," he assured
J. A. Symonds in 1886.
Stevenson was twenty-four when Leslie Stephen

took him to the Edinburgh Infirmary to see a
" poor sort of poet who writes for him," and
Henley was twenty-six. It is not easy to estimate
how far Henley affected Stevenson's artistic development. The faults of style pilloried by his
later critics he shares with Henley, and I think
that Mr. Chesterton is right when he suggests that
it was due to Henley that Stevenson sometimes
invites his readers to admire brutality when he
thinks he is inviting them to admire masculine
courage.

Certainly Henley's review of Sir Graham
Balfour's *Life* suggests the complete failure to
understand his friend. It also suggests the gnaw-
ing jealousy of one sick man of another's more
comfortable bed and more affectionate friends.
Stevenson was sometimes a cad, Henley says.
There is no alternative word of three letters, as
Mrs. Meynell discovered. The truth is, that
Stevenson was a casuist, and Henley could never
understand casuistry.

" A man is not to expect happiness," Stevenson
wrote in *A Christmas Sermon*. " Why not ? "
Henley would certainly have demanded. " The
man who cannot forgive any mortal thing is a
green hand in life," Stevenson wrote in *Prince
Otto*. " Slopppy rubbish," Henley would have
commented.

Stevenson grieved at the loss of Henley. He
would, if he could, have kept both wife and friend.

Henley, too, in his own way, sorrowed for his friend. In 1891 he wrote the poem in which are the lines :

O, we that were dear, we are all-too-near
With the thick of the world between us.

But six years later the notorious article appeared in the *Pall Mall Magazine*, " the assassin article," as Mrs. Meynell called it. Henley could never forgive.

Mrs. Stevenson telegraphed from San Francisco that the yacht *Casco* might be chartered for a voyage in the Pacific. The *Casco* was a racing schooner with graceful lines and elaborate fittings, but none too seaworthy, and the charter cost Stevenson two thousand pounds of the three thousand which he had inherited from his father. " If this business fails to set me up," he wrote to England, " well, two thousand pounds is gone and I know that I can't get better." Stevenson took over the skipper, the Chinese cook, and the crew—three Swedes and a Finn. The Stevensons left New York on June 7th, and they sailed from San Francisco on June 28th. Stevenson wrote to Henry James :

" This, dear James, is a valedictory. On June 15th the schooner yacht *Casco* will (weather and a jealous providence permitting) steam through the Golden Gates for Honolulu, Tahiti, the Galapagos, Guayaquil, and—I hope *not* the bottom of the Pacific. It will contain your obedient 'umble servant and party. It seems too good to be true, and is a very good way of getting through the green-sickness of maturity, which, with all its accompanying ills, is now declaring itself in my mind and life."

CHAPTER X

THE SETTING SUN

THE cruise of the *Casco*, a small vessel of seventy-four tons register, lasted for about six months. Stevenson was radiantly happy. There was for him an immense attraction in the colour and romance of the Pacific Islands. But, for his wife, the voyage was another purgatory. She was always a bad sailor, and she said in a letter to Mrs. Sitwell : " To keep house on a yacht is no easy matter. When I was deathly sick the question was put to me by the cook : ' What shall we have for the cabin dinner, what for to-morrow's breakfast, what for lunch, and what about the sailors' food ? And please come and look at the biscuits, for the weevils have got into them, and show me how to make yeast that will rise of itself, and smell the pork, which seems pretty high, and give me directions about making a pudding with molasses, etc.' In the midst of heavy dangerous weather, when I was lying on the floor in utter misery, down comes the mate with a cracked head, and I must needs cut off the blood-clotted hair, wash and dress the wound,

and administer restoratives.   I do not like being
the ' lady of the yacht.' " [1]

Even for Stevenson the Pacific sometimes lost
its glamour.   " The sea," he said in a letter to
Sidney Colvin, " is a terrible place, stupefying to
the mind and poisonous to the temper.   The
motion, the lack of space, the cruel publicity, the
villainous tinned foods, the sailors, the captain,
the passengers."   But he added :   " You are
amply repaid when you sight an island and drop
anchor in a new world."

The " new world " in which they dropped
anchor on the 28th July 1888 was the group of
islands called the Marquesas, some three thousand
miles from the American coast, where the white
man was then comparatively unknown, though the
port, Nukahiva, is mentioned in Herman Melville's
Typee.   Melville found the Marquesas disap-
pointing.   He says :   " Bold rock-bound coasts,
with the surf beating high against the lofty cliffs,
and broken here and there into deep inlets, which
open to the view thickly wooded valleys, separated by the spurs of mountains clothed with tufted
grass, and sweeping down towards the sea from an
elevated and furrowed interior, form the principal features of these islands."   But Stevenson was
thrilled.   In a magnificent piece of descriptive writing in the first chapter of *In the South Seas*, he says:
" The land heaved up in peaks and rising vales ;

[1] *Life of Mrs. R. L. Stevenson*, by N. V. de G. Sanchez, p. 136.

it fell in cliffs and buttresses ; its colour ran
through fifty modulations in a scale of pearl and
rose and olive ; and it was crowned above by
opalescent clouds. The suffusion of vague hues
deceived the eye ; the shadows of clouds were
confounded with the articulations of the mountain ; and the isle and its unsubstantial canopy
rose and shimmered before us like a single mass.
There was no beacon, no smoke of towns to be
expected, no plying pilot."

The one English trader on the island came
aboard the *Casco* with a native chief, " both in
immaculate white European clothes," and soon
the yacht was overrun with " stalwart six-foot
men in every stage of undress." Melville said of
the people of the Marquesas that " so far as re-
gards their peculiar customs and general mode of
life, they retained their original primitive character, remaining very nearly in the same state of
nature in which they were first beheld by white
men." The people remained much the same
when Stevenson landed. Probably nowadays
they are well provided with gramophones and
the wireless.

Stevenson preened himself that he was a cosmopolitan. He professed to be more at home in
France than in Scotland. But in the South Seas
he felt himself for the first time among people,
strange and hardly to be understood—" beyond
the reach of articulate communication, like furred

animals, or folk born deaf, or the dwellers of some
alien planet." He was incapable of the vulgarity
of race superiority. He was ready enough to be
friends, but at the beginning he was bewildered
and apparently a little terrified. As they stayed
on the island, he was first interested and then
delighted by the climate, and afterwards by the
people. Mrs. Stevenson learned native cooking,
and Stevenson made friends. He wrote to Sidney
Colvin :

" I know one old chief Ko-o-amua, a great
cannibal in his day, who ate his enemies even as
he walked home from killing 'em, and he is a
perfect gentleman and exceedingly amiable and
simple-minded : no fool, though."

The Stevensons were in the Marquesas Islands
until September 4th, when they sailed for Tahiti,
through what is known as the Dangerous Archipelago, having first shipped a mate who was
familiar with the waters, and a Chinese cook, Ah
Fu, who was to remain with them, a devoted servant, for two years. On September 9th they
arrived at the island of Fakarava, " after a very
difficult and dangerous passage." Here they
stayed for some time. The days were very hot,
but the evenings were cool, and they made great
friends with the half-caste Resident of the island.
Mrs. Stevenson and her mother-in-law learned
from the natives how to make plaited hats out
of bamboo shavings. Stevenson was happy

and sunburned : " Only my trunk and the aristocratic spot on which I sit, retain the vile whiteness of the north," he wrote to Colvin. Mrs. Stevenson has described their days in Fakarava :

" Leaving the yacht *Casco* in the lagoon, we hired a cottage on the beach where we lived for several weeks. Fakarava is an atoll of the usual horseshoe shape, so narrow that one can walk across it in ten minutes, but of great circumference ; it lay so little above the sea level that one had a sense of insecurity, justified by the terrible disasters following the last hurricane in the group. Not far from where we lived the waves had recently swept over the narrow strip of coral during a storm. Our life passed in a gentle monotony of peace. At sunrise we walked from our front door into the warm shallow waters of the lagoon for our bath ; we cooked our breakfast on the remains of an old American cooking stove I discovered on the beach, and spent the rest of the morning sorting over the shells we had found the previous day. After lunch and a siesta, we crossed the island to the windward side and gathered more shells. Sometimes we would find the strangest fish stranded in pools between the rocks by the outgoing tide, many of them curiously shaped and brilliantly coloured. Some of the most gorgeous were poisonous to eat, and capable of inflicting very unpleasant wounds with their fins. The captain suffered for a long time with a sort of paralysis in a finger he had scratched when handling a fish with a beak like a parrot." [1]

From Fakarava they went on to Papeete, the capital of Tahiti, where Stevenson was taken very ill. Realising that the place did not agree with him, Mrs. Stevenson insisted once more on going to sea, and skirting the island in what turned out to be a singularly perilous voyage, they landed at Taravao on its south side and journeyed inland sixteen miles to Tautira, Stevenson travelling in a cart and sustained by small doses of coca. Here they found a house and received unbounded kindness from a Tahitian princess, and from Ori, the chief of the village.

It had been discovered that the *Casco* was dangerously unseaworthy, and, while it was sent back to Papeete for repairs, the Stevensons remained at Tautira, very content with their native friends, in a settlement where the only other Europeans were a French gendarme and a Dutch priest. It was, Sir Graham Balfour says, one of the happiest periods in Stevenson's life. The chief, Ori, was " exactly like a colonel in the Guards ; a great gentleman, and the kindest and the most sympathetic of friends," and Tautira itself was " the garden of the world." Stevenson started work again and almost finished *The Master of Ballantrae*

1 *Life of Mrs. R. L. Stevenson*, by N. V. de G. Sanchez, p. 140.

He began to write his Pacific Island ballads which Sidney Colvin admits that he never very much admired, " thinking them unequal and uncertain both in metre and in style."

The *Song of Rahero* is dedicated to Ori :

Ori, my brother in the island mode,
In every tongue and meaning much my friend,
This story of your country and your clan,
In your loved house, your too much honoured guest,
  made in English. Take it, being done ;
And let me sign it with the name you gave.

Stevenson made friends easily and pleasantly exaggerated the depth and intensity of his friendships.

In every tongue and meaning much my friend

is much to say of a man of an entirely different race and tradition whom he had only known for a few weeks, though Ori certainly gave him sufficient reason for gratitude and hyperbole.

Stevenson gained in health every day : " He takes sea baths and swims," his wife wrote, " and lives almost entirely in the open air as nearly without clothes as possible." But their money and their stores began to run out, and the *Casco* was an unconscionable time in being refitted. Their chief friend did not fail them : " You are my brother," he said to Stevenson, " all that I have is yours. I know that your food is done, but I can give you plenty of fish and taro. We like you and wish to have you here. Stay where you are till the *Casco* comes. Be happy, *ne pleurez pas.*"

After two months the *Casco* reappeared, and the Stevensons set sail for Honolulu, which they reached after another troublesome voyage of thirty days. At this time, Stevenson was contemplating a return to England directly he had paid the expenses of the cruise from the moneys that he was to receive from the account he was writing of it. For the moment his finances were low.

With all its inconveniences and occasional peril, he had immensely enjoyed this first stage of his island voyage, and was hungry for more. The elder Mrs. Stevenson had to return to Scotland, but her son and daughter-in-law decided to remain for a while in the Pacific. *The Master of Ballantrae* was finished soon after the arrival in Honolulu, where the *Casco* was dismissed and where they proposed to remain until the spring. It was apparently not till after the safe arrival in Honolulu that Stevenson realised how dangerous the *Casco* trip had been. He wrote to his cousin :

" We had a very small schooner, and like most yachts, over-rigged and over-sparred, and like many American yachts, on a very dangerous sail plan. The waters sailed in are, of course, entirely unlighted, and very badly charted ; in the Dangerous Archipelago, through which we were fools enough to go, we were perfectly in ignorance

of where we were for a whole night and half the
next day, and this in the midst of invisible islands
and rapid and variable currents ; and we were
lucky when we found our whereabouts at last."

During the last part of the voyage they had
faced hurricane weather on an unseaworthy
vessel, but Stevenson said : " The perils of the
deep were part of the programme, and though I
am very glad to be done with them for a while
and comfortably ashore where a squall does not
matter a snuff to anyone, I feel pretty sure I shall
want to go to sea again ere long." His health
was wonderful. He had accumulated material
for a book. He had had new and exciting
experiences. The adventurer was satisfied.

Mrs. Stevenson's daughter was living in
Honolulu, and this provided them with a circle
of interesting acquaintance. They lived in a
rambling house outside the town, and Stevenson
was able to do a good deal of work, properly irritating his wife by attempting a sort of scientific
study of the South Seas, instead of busying himself with romance and adventure. Sir Graham
Balfour has insisted that his cousin's knowledge of the South Sea islands was accurate and
extensive, but his wife knew that the last thing
that his public wanted from him was a glorified
guide-book. " What a thing it is to have a man of
genius to deal with," she said in a letter to Sidney
Colvin, " it is like managing an over-bred horse."

They remained in Honolulu until the summer of 1889, Stevenson spending part of his time in studying the Hawaiian language. He was troubled neither by cough nor hemorrhage. " I have had more fun and pleasure in my life these past months than ever before, and more health than any time in ten long years," he wrote to Henry James, and he professed that if his books had done nothing more than enable him to make the Pacific voyage, they had not been written in vain.

In May, Stevenson made a trip by himself to Molokai, the leper colony where Father Damien had lived and laboured, and where he had died a week or two before Stevenson's visit. The leper settlement was " a little town of wooden houses, two churches, a landing stair, all unsightly, sour, northerly, lying athwart the sunrise, with the great wall of the pali cutting the world out on the south." The lepers seemed to him " pantomime masks in poor human flesh." But when he had landed among them " all horror was quite gone from me. To see these dreadful creatures smile and look happy was beautiful." And in a letter to Colvin he said : " The sight of so much courage, cheerfulness, and devotion stung me too high to mind the infinite pity and horror of the sights." He at once conceived an immense admiration for Father Damien, whom he was soon to defend with magnificent invective. He was "a peasant, dirty, bigoted, untruthful, unwise, tricky, but superb in generosity, residual candour, and fundamental good humour."

There was among the lepers a general revolt against enforced segregation, and there were continual attempts to escape from the colony, inspired by the yearning for the family, a characteristic of the South Sea islanders. But in his letters, and in the papers written afterwards in Vailima, Stevenson notes that, after a while, the lepers accepted the not altogether uncomfortable circumstances of the colony's life, and were happy and even gay and indifferent to what to the clean man is a horrible and loathsome disease. Arrived in the lazaretto " they were strangers to each other, collected by common calamity, disfigured, mortally sick, banished without sin from home and friends." They were supported by the Government, pauperised, diseased, but still capable of enjoyment ; and Stevenson has written what he calls Damien's picture of the settlement— " Cards, dancing and debauch were the diversions ; the women served as prostitutes ; the children as drudges ; the dying were callously uncared for ; heathenism revived ; *okolehau* was brewed and in their orgies the disfigured sick ran naked by the sea." Stevenson notes that crime was practically unknown in the settlement, and " on the whole the spectacle of life in this marred and moribund community, with its idleness, its furnished table, its horse riding, music and gallantries, under the shadow of death, confounds the expectations of the visitor." He was particularly interested in a home for leper children run by a Roman Catholic Sisterhood, and after his return to Honolulu he sent the home a present of a grand piano.

But it was Father Damien far more than the lepers who attracted him. He was convinced that the Belgian priest was "a man with all the grime and paltriness of mankind, but a saint and hero all the more for that." After he had left Honolulu he read the attack on Father Damien written by the Rev. C. M. Hyde, a Protestant missionary in Honolulu, and printed in a paper called *The Presbyterian*, published in Sydney. The result was the famous "open letter" which, in its righteous abuse, has few equals in literature. The Protestant missionary, living in a sumptuous house in Honolulu, and sneering at the old Catholic priest in his dirty hut in the leper settlement, was too much for Stevenson's stomach, and he let himself go with a relish. Among the other charges made by the Presbyterian gentleman was that Damien was not a pure man in his relations with women. Stevenson recalls that he heard the same charge made in a bar-room by a "miserable leering creature," who was hotly denounced by another of the beachcombing drinkers. " If the story were a thousand times true, can't you see you are a million times lower for daring to repeat it ? " Stevenson concludes :

" You had a father : suppose this tale were about him, and some informant brought it to you, proof in hand : I am not making too high an estimate of your emotional nature when I suppose you would regret the circumstance ? that you should feel the tale of frailty the more keenly since it shamed the author of your days ? and that the last thing you would do would be to publish it in the religious press ? Well, the man who tried to do what Damien did, is my father, and the father of the man in the Apia bar, and the father of all who love goodness ; and he was your father too, if God had given you grace to see it."

The publication of this letter has been regretted, even by some of Stevenson's most fervent eulogists. " It is a matchless piece of scorn and invective," wrote Walter Raleigh, " not inferior in skill to anything he ever wrote. But that it was well done is no proof that it should have been done at all."[1] But the letter was surely characteristic of Stevenson's chivalry. A sick man, he had an instinctive sympathy with all other sick men, even though their sickness was loathsome—this, by the way, is by no means common—and, to him, Father Damien was the Good Samaritan whose shortcomings were to be forgotten, and who was to be remembered and admired since he had

[1] *R. L. Stevenson*, by Walter Raleigh, p. 44.

ministered to the man who had fallen among
thieves, "bound up his wounds, pouring in oil
and wine, and set him on his own beast, and
brought him to an inn, and took care of him."

Besides his visit to the leper settlement, Stevenson made other excursions among the islands
during his stay in Honolulu, busy collecting
material for the South Sea essays.

His mother left for Scotland in May, and in
June the Stevensons, with Mrs. Stevenson's son-
in-law, sailed from Honolulu in the *Equator*, a
schooner of sixty-four tons register.   In a letter to
Sidney Colvin, dated May 21st, Mrs. Stevenson
says : "A trading schooner, the *Equator*, will come
along some time in the first part of June, lie outside the harbour here and signal to us.   Within
forty-eight hours we shall pack up our posses-
sions, our barrel of *sauerkraut*, our barrel of salt
onions, our bag of cocoanuts, our native garments,
our tobacco, fish hooks, red combs, and Turkey-
red calicoes (all the latter for trading purposes),
our hand organ, photograph and painting
materials, and finally our magic lantern—all
these upon a large whaleboat, and go out to the
Equator.   Lloyd, also, takes a fiddle, a guitar, a
native instrument something like a banjo, called
a taropatch fiddle, and a lot of song books.   We
shall be carried first to one of the Gilberts, landing at Butaritari.   The *Equator* is going about
amongst the Gilbert group, and we have the right

to keep her over when we like within reasonable
limits. Finally she will leave us, and we shall
have to take the chances of what happens next.
We hope to see the Marshalls, the Carolines,
the Fijis, Tonga and Samoa (also other islands
that I do not remember), perhaps staying a
little while in Sydney, and stopping on our way
home to see our friends in Tahiti and the
Marquesas."

This second of the Pacific voyages lasted six
months, and plans were considerably modified
before it came to an end. " This cruise is up to
now a huge success, being interesting, pleasant,
and profitable," Stevenson wrote at the end of
August. The people of the Marshall Islands were
a very different type to the Polynesians, whom
Stevenson had met in Honolulu and the Marquesas and Tahiti, and whom he was to know
more intimately in Samoa. They are a mixed
race with a definitely Mongol appearance, and
almost certainly with a certain proportion of
Japanese blood. Stevenson found them " moral,
stand-offish (for good reasons), and protected by a
dark tongue." He was glad to meet Hawaiian
missionaries, who were always very friendly, and
he was immensely interested in the villainous
beachcombers. " One, the only undoubted assassin of the lot, quite gained my affection in his
big home out of a wreck, with his New Hebrides
wife in her savage turban of hair and yet a perfect

lady, and his three adorable little girls in Rob Roy
Macgregor dresses dancing to the hand organ,
performing circus on the floor with startling effects
of nudity, and curling up together on a mat to
sleep, three sizes, three attitudes, three Rob Roy
dresses, and six little clenched fists ; the murderer
meanwhile brooding and gloating over his chicks,
till your whole heart went out to him ; and yet
his crime on the face of it was dark ; disembowel-
ling, in his own house, an old man of seventy, and
him drunk.''

A new literary project was launched during the
voyage. As a consequence of meeting the beachcombers, Stevenson and Lloyd Osbourne had
begun to work out the plot of *The Wrecker*. It
was to be written at once and sent to a publisher
from Samoa, and with the proceeds they were to
buy a schooner, and Stevenson was to start life
again as a Pacific Island trader. This was one of
the many schemes which he loved to work out in
elaborate detail. None of them came to anything. He probably never supposed that they
would, but it was great fun to make plans ahead,
and the more fantastic the plans, the greater the
fun. Stevenson was of one mind with Ibsen's
Master Builder that the happiest homes in the
world are the castles in the air.

Some weeks before writing the letter from which
I have just quoted, the Stevensons landed at the
town of Butaritari, in the island of Nakin, the

most northerly of the Marshalls, which Stevenson
has described as " warrens of men ruled over with
some rustic pomp." It had been arranged that
they should stay for some weeks at Butaritari
while the *Equator* was trading with the neigh-
bouring islands.

They arrived at an unfortunate time. The
traders and the missionaries in Butaritari were
American, and to celebrate the 4th July, in
honour of his foreign friends, the King had removed the taboo from the drinking of spirits,
with the consequence that the whole town became
gloriously drunk, and was still gloriously drunk,
when the Stevensons landed nine days later. The
visitors were in some danger. The King, a tall,
fat, timorous man, who " seemed at once op-
pressed with drowsiness and held awake by appre-
hension," was told that Stevenson was Queen
Victoria's nephew, and that there would be
dreadful trouble if anything serious happened to
him. He promised to put back the taboo on
spirits, but as he had been spending days drinking kümmel out of tumblers, it was not unnatural
that the promise was broken, and the debauch
was only brought to an end when Stevenson persuaded the traders to take the risk of having their
bar-rooms raided and to refuse to serve the natives
with any more drink. Sir Graham Balfour says
that, when the carouse had come to an end, the
Stevensons found Butaritari rather dull, but that

is certainly not the impression derived from Stevenson's own narrative.

He and his family lived in the house of a Hawaiian missionary—" I have never known a more engaging preacher than this parson of Butaritari "—who treated them with the greatest kindness and hospitality. They regularly accompanied their host to church on Sunday, " the missionary a blot on the hot landscape, being clothed in tall hat, frock coat and black trousers." His congregation never consisted of more than thirty persons, and Stevenson had never heard worse hymn-singing. During the sermon the congregation for the most part slept, and Stevenson himself found it tremendously difficult to keep awake. But his admiration for the missionary remained—a man with no cakes and ale in his life, with nothing but toil and church-going. At the same time, it seemed to Stevenson a little ironic that Christian missionaries should travel from Honolulu to the Marshall Islands " from a country recklessly unchaste to one conspicuously strict."

Far more amusing than the church was the bar-room, where of a night the local traders and a ship's captain or two made up the usual company. With the exception of one black sheep, a beachcomber, of singular degradation, Stevenson found them gay and genial and gallant. But the most interesting person on the island was the royal interpreter, an American negro and a runaway ship's cook. " I never knew a man who had more words in his command or less truth to communicate." The native wives, too, of the white traders were a source of wonder and amusement. These ladies had a far greater freedom than their sisters. All the marriages were regarded as legitimate, and the certificates were carefully preserved, though one certificate, which of course the lady could not read, announced that she was married for one night and that in the morning her husband could " send her to hell." Another native wife had been solemnly married on a pirated edition of one of Stevenson's own books.

From Butaritari the Stevensons sailed southward to the large island of Apemama, where generally white men were not allowed to land. But the chief, Tembinoka, visited the ship and, after two days' reflection, the Stevensons were welcomed as his personal guests. Houses were prepared for them, and they stayed on the island for six weeks, eventually establishing intimate personal friendship with the chief. Stevenson has described his stay in Apemama in what Sidney Colvin considered the most interesting and attractive chapters of *In the South Seas*. Tembinoka was one of the last of the Pacific Island tyrants. The Marshalls are now under British tutelage with a British Resident and organised government, but the old government was at least effective. The

King, a man of force and character, was both the sole ruler and the sole trader. " He had a beaked profile like Dante's in the mask, a mane of long black hair, the eye brilliant, imperious and enquiring." He was sometimes dressed in naval uniform, sometimes in a woman's frock, sometimes in garments of green velvet or red silk designed by himself to please his own royal taste. He had all the savage potentate's appetite for the collecting of useless European and American productions, and his houses were crammed with musical boxes, sewing machines, and other such contraptions.

Before the Stevensons were allowed to stay in his town, they had solemnly to promise never to give any of his subjects liquor, money, or tobacco. Settled in their new and quite comfortable house, Stevenson was busy hammering out *The Wrecker* with Lloyd Osbourne. With Lloyd Osbourne, too, he began *The Pearl Fisher*, which afterwards was called *The Ebb Tide*, and the essays in *In the South Seas* were sketched out and a synopsis sent to Sidney Colvin.

He read Gibbon and Carlyle, and in leisure moments strummed on a guitar, took photographs and played patience. They were living among a happy people, orderly, sober, and innocent. Life passed on the island from day to day, as on a model plantation under a model planter. There were no crime, no drunkenness, no anxiety. The people were superstitious, and had largely lapsed into paganism, and even the priests of the gods were the slaves of the masterful and stubborn king. Tembinoka was heartbroken when his guests departed. " The King took us on board in his own gig, dressed on the occasion in a naval uniform. He had little to say, he refused refreshment, shook us briefly by the hand and went ashore again." Stevenson was to meet Tembinoka once more, and he always counted him among his best friends. He wrote :

" The King is a great character—a thorough tyrant, very much of a gentleman, a poet, a musician, a historian, or perhaps rather more a genealogist—it is strange to see him lying in his house among a lot of wives (nominal wives) writing the History of Apemama in an account-book ; his description of one of his own songs, which he sang to me himself, as ' about sweethearts, and trees, and the sea—and no true, all-the-same lie,' seems about as compendious a definition of lyric poetry as a man could ask. Tembinoka is here the great attraction : all the rest is heat and tedium and villainous dazzle, and yet more villainous mosquitoes."

With all the incidental discomfort, Stevenson was buoyantly happy : " Life is far better fun than people dream who fall asleep among the chimney stacks and telegraph wires." From Apemama the *Equator* sailed south-east to Samoa, again experiencing the worst possible weather.

Stevenson wrote to his mother : " We were sixteen souls in this small schooner, eleven in the
cabin ; our confinement and overcrowding in the
wet weather was excessive ; we lost our foretop-
mast in a squall ; the sails were continually being
patched (we had but the one suit), and with all
attention we lost the jibtopsail almost entirely
and the staysail and mainsail are far through."

His thirty-ninth birthday was celebrated during
this stormy voyage. Mrs. Stevenson and her son
wrote a song, *On Board the Old " Equator,"* specially
for the occasion, and it was sung by Paul Hoflich,
a German trader who was travelling with them.
Hoflich wrote to Mr. Stevenson's sister twenty-
seven years afterwards :

" As I look back now I cannot help admiring
Mrs. Stevenson for her bravery and endurance in
her resolution to remain with her husband. For
us men this life was right enough, but for a refined
woman it meant great hardship. When Mr.
Stevenson, in his birthday speech on board, said
with moist eyes that he had never enjoyed a
voyage and company so well as ours, Mrs. Stevenson deserved the largest share of that praise. I
remember how she took care of him." [1]

Stevenson was still planning far ahead. He
told Colvin that he expected to be in England in
the following June. " I can hear the rattle of the
hansom up Endell Street." And to James Payn

[1] *Life of Mrs. R. L. Stevenson*, by N. V. de G. Sanchez, p. 161.

he wrote : " Some time in the month of June a stalwart weather-beaten man, evidently of sea-faring antecedents, shall be observed wending his way between the Athenæum Club and Waterloo Place." It was not until some months later that he was compelled to accept the inevitable and to give up all idea of returning home.

The *Equator* arrived at Apia, the capital of Upolu, the most important of the Samoan Islands, on December 7th, and the Stevensons landed with the idea of staying there for about two months. Before his arrival, Stevenson had already decided to add a section on Samoa to his South Sea studies, confining himself to the history of the civil war which had prevailed during 1887 and 1888, and in which the British, American, and German Governments had been concerned. A treaty guaranteeing the independence of the islands was signed by the three Powers at Berlin six months before Stevenson's arrival. Stevenson lived at Apia in the house of an American trader, and he took immense pains to arrive at the facts contained in his *A Footnote to History*, the reliability of which, as Sir Graham Balfour has said, has never been questioned. He had interviews with the English and the German Consuls, he made friends with missionaries, he had long talks with Mataafa, the chief, who had been supported by Great Britain and the United States, but who was deposed by the Treaty of Berlin, whom he found " a fine fellow, plenty sense, and the most dignified, quiet, gentle manners."

" I am not specially attracted by the people," he wrote to his friend Charles Baxter, " but they are courteous, the women very attractive and dressed lovely ; the men purpose-like, well set up, tall, lean and dignified."

Mr. Lloyd Osbourne has described the idyllic life of Samoa :

" The native life of Samoa is more similar to that of the ancient Greeks than any other we have ever known on this planet ; there is the same love of physical perfection, of beauty, of pageantry. The Samoans are extraordinarily good-looking, with gracious manners and an innate love of what for lack of a better term I will call ' good form.' To fail in any of the little courtesies of life is to write oneself down a boor. Every public event —no matter how trivial—takes place with singing, with flowers, with processions, with an immemorial art in which beauty and grouping has been as much studied as in any performance of the Russian ballet, though less self-consciously.

" Samoans, both men and women, all go bareheaded and half-naked ; and the feeling that you are in ancient Greece thus becomes intensified as you gaze at those bronze Apollos, those lovely, slender girls with their breasts scarcely concealed by garlands, those superb old men, noble foils to all this glowing youth, leaning on their staves and booming out their orations. It is a poetic life ; the appeal to your sense of beauty is incessant, and the language, soft and melodious, is in harmony with such a people. Ulysses could land here to-morrow and feel at home." [1]

As in other of the islands, Stevenson made friends with the beachcombers, that strange colony of whites and half whites, the majority of them morally and financially derelict.

The civil war in Samoa has to-day little historic interest. The conditions of the islands have been immensely affected by the events that have happened since Stevenson's death and, of course, by the Great War. But *A Footnote to History* is interesting because of its balanced judgments. Here, for once, Stevenson is the historian and not the partisan. As he says in one of his letters : " The Germans have behaved pretty badly here, but not in all ways so ill as you may have gathered. They were doubtless much provoked."

While he was in Apia, Stevenson made two expeditions, one to the east and another to the west, and it was on one of these trips that, for the first time, he received the native name of *Tusitala*, " the Writer of Tales." It was during these expeditions that he fell in love with the country and the people. One place he visited was, he said, " the original spot where every prospect pleases," and he determined to have a permanent winter

[1] *Samoa under the Sailing Gods*, by N. A. Rowe, Introd., pp. xii, xiv.

home in Samoa, purchasing three hundred acres —the estate now known to all the world as Vailima—in the bush, two miles from Apia.

His experiences since he left Sydney had convinced him that, if he was to live in the Pacific Isles, it must be somewhere within touch of his publishers. Mail steamers from both Australia and the United States regularly called at Apia, and for this reason alone Stevenson regarded it as a suitable home. At Apia, he received the English reviews of *The Master of Ballantrae*, most of which were extremely laudatory, though he was annoyed and perhaps a little hurt to know that Henley had described it as " grimy." " Grim it is, God knows, but sure not grimy, else I am the more deceived."

Before finally settling in Samoa, the Stevensons returned to Sydney, where he printed his vehement defence of Father Damien—it was afterwards published in the *Scots Observer*—and then was taken so ill with fever and hemorrhage that the scheme for a return to England for the summer had to be abandoned. " I am sure I shall never come back home except to die," he wrote to Baxter. " I may do it, but shall always think of the move as suicidal unless a great change comes over me, of which as yet I see no symptom." He wrote to Colvin : " So soon as I cease from cruising, the nerves are strained, the decline commences, and I steer slowly but surely back

to bedward." With some considerable difficulty
Mrs. Stevenson obtained berths on the *Janet
Nicoll*, which was about to start for the islands.
" There 's no use in trying to blink the fact that
the *Janet* is a pig," Stevenson said, " I never saw
such a roller." But the officers were a pleasant
company, and one of them became the original
of Tommy Haddon in *The Wrecker*. He wrote to
Colvin :

" After a day in Auckland, we set sail again ;
were blown up in the main cabin with calcium
fires, as we left the bay. Let no man say I am
unscientific : when I ran, on the alert, out of my
state-room, and found the main cabin incarnadined with the glow of the last scene of a pantomime, I stopped dead : ' What is this ? ' said I.
' This ship is on fire, I see that ; but why a
pantomime ? ' And I stood and reasoned the
point, until my head was so muddled with the
fumes that I could not find the companion. A
few seconds later, the captain had to enter crawl-
ing on his belly, and took days to recover (if he
has recovered) from the fumes. By singular good
fortune, we got the hose down in time and saved
the ship, but Lloyd lost most of his clothes and a
great part of our photographs were destroyed.
Fanny saw the native sailors tossing overboard a
blazing trunk ; she stopped them in time, and
behold it contained my manuscripts."

The Stevensons stayed for a few days in Apia

P

to see how the building of their house was proceeding, put in at Apemama where their old friend, King Tembinoka, was in bad trouble, his people suffering from an epidemic of measles, and Stevenson landed by himself in the French penal colony at Noumea. He was ill again on this voyage, the stuffy cabins being difficult to endure. This journey on a fast steamer was far less beneficial to his health than the buffeting that he had experienced in more or less crazy tubs. He arrived at Noumea, " very seedy, utterly fatigued, and overborne with sleep." After a short visit, he went on to Sydney, where his wife and stepson were waiting for him, Lloyd Osbourne going from there to England to settle up the family affairs and to bring the furniture from Bournemouth to Samoa. " Pray keep him in funds, if I have any," Stevenson wrote to Baxter, " if I have not, pray try to raise them." He wrote to Henry James :

" I must tell you plainly—I can't tell Colvin— I do not think I shall come to England more than once, and then it 'll be to die. Health I enjoy in the tropics ; even here, which they call sub- or semi-tropics, I come only to catch cold. I have not been out since my arrival ; live here in a nice bedroom by the fireside, and read books and letters from Henry James, and send out to get his *Tragic Muse*, only to be told they can't be had as yet in Sydney, and have altogether a placid time. But I can't go out! The thermometer was nearly down to 50° the other day—no temperature for me, Mr. James : how should I do in England ? I fear not at all. Am I very sorry ? I am sorry about seven or eight people in England, and one or two in the States. And outside that, I simply prefer Samoa."

He read Kipling, whom he found " too clever to live," Zola's *La Bête Humaine*, which he hated, and Hall Caine's *The Bondman*, which he liked very much.

He was back again in Samoa with his wife in November 1890. " We live here in a beautiful land amid a beautiful and interesting people," he wrote. " The life is still very hard : my wife and I live in a two-roomed cottage about three miles from and six hundred and fifty feet above the sea ; we have had to make the road to it ; our supplies are very imperfect ; in the wild weather of this (the hurricane) season we have much discomfort ; one night the wind blew in our house so outrageously that we must sit in the dark ; and as the sound of rain on the roof made speech inaudible, you may imagine we found the evening long. All these things, however, are pleasant to me."

In these early weeks he seems to have felt something of the loneliness of exile. Letters were few and far between, a great many of them seemed to have been lost in transit, and in the months while they were waiting for the arrival of Lloyd Osbourne and the furniture from England, Stevenson and his wife lived "like the family after a sale." But the sheer beauty of Vailima was sufficient compensation : " The place is beautiful beyond dreams ; some fifty miles of the Pacific spread in front ; deep woods all round ; a mountain making in the sky a profile of huge trees upon our left."

He was working on his South Sea essays, realising that those of them that he had written on board the *Janet Nicoll* needed a great deal of rewriting. Sidney Colvin had no very high regard for these essays, but Joseph Conrad preferred them even to *Treasure Island*.

In January 1891 Stevenson returned to Sydney to meet his mother, who was coming back to him from Scotland. In Australia he was again very ill and unable to work. He was able, however, to take his mother back to Samoa, where she only made a short stay, as the house was not ready for her reception, returning to Australia for a couple of months, and finally settling in Samoa in the April, " young, well and in good spirits." Stevenson said of her :

> *The old lady* (so they say), but I
> Admire your young vitality,
> Still brisk of foot, still busy and keen
> In and about and up and down.

By this time the house had been largely rebuilt.

" We have spent since we have been here about
£2500, which is not much if you consider we have
built on that three houses, one of them of some
size, and a considerable stable, made two miles of
road some three times, cleared many acres of
bush, made some miles of path, planted quanti-
ties of food, and enclosed a horse paddock and
some acres of pig run ; but 'tis a good deal of
money regarded simply as money."

Stevenson was now busy with *The Beach of
Falesa*, which he described as a " fable too fantastic and far-fetched." Walter Raleigh admired " the racy humorous and imaginative
slang " of the best of Stevenson's later work. His
application and persistence were almost comparable to those of Anthony Trollope. He wrote
steadily, day after day, at least two thousand
words, which he well described as " the labours
of an elephant."

In the summer he was very far from well, unfit
for work, incapable of much reading, but he was
interested and happy. He formed a sort of
family band—the flageolet, flute, clarinet, and
piano—and he had become immensely interested
and a good deal bothered by local politics, which
Sidney Colvin confesses that he found parochial
and dull. "The natives," Stevenson wrote, "have
been scurvily used by all the white powers without exception, and they labour under the belief,
of which they can't be cured, that they defeated

Germany. This makes an awkward complication." White officials were well meaning but incompetent, and Stevenson became the steady critic of the form of government sanctioned by the Treaty of Berlin.

As *The Beach of Falesa* grew under his hand, his doubts about it entirely disappeared. " Golly, it's good," he wrote. " I am not shining by modesty ; but I do just love the colour and movement of that piece so far as it goes." He reported to Colvin : " I have written and re-written *The Beach of Falesa*, something like sixty thousand words of sterling domestic fiction." He believed that this was " the first realistic South Sea story that had been written in English," and he assured Colvin that he would know more about the South Seas " after you have read my little tale, than if you had read a library." In October he began to write *Catriona*, the second part of *Kidnapped*. *The Wrecker* was finished in the middle of November, and he considered it " a long tough yarn with some pictures of the manners of to-day in the greater world—not the shoddy, sham world of city clubs and colleges, the world where men still live a man's life."

He remained keenly concerned with public affairs, and his position was not altogether comfortable. He was popular with the natives, and, perhaps for that reason, unpopular with the Germans. In addition to his other books, he was working hard at the end of 1891 and the beginning of 1892 on his *A Footnote to History*, the story of Samoa, which he quite reasonably doubted whether any one would read. But with all this activity he was restless at the comparative paucity of his literary output :

" How do journalists fetch up their drivel ? I aim only at clearness and the most obvious finish, positively at no higher degree of merit, not even at brevity—I am sure it could not have been all done, with double the time, in two-thirds of the space. And yet it has taken me two months to write 45,000 words ; and, be damned to my wicked prowess, I am proud of the exploit ! The real journalist must be a man not of brass only, but bronze."

At the beginning of 1892, Stevenson was down with influenza, but before the summer he had finished *A Footnote to History*, had planned a South Sea novel, which was never written, and added many chapters to *Catriona*. By the end of the year, he had also begun *Weir of Hermiston*. During the year, the Stevensons were joined by Graham Balfour, a cousin whom Stevenson had apparently never before met, who was to become his close intimate and, subsequently, his biographer.

The trouble with the local authorities led to a threat of deportation which was probably never serious. As a matter of fact, the publication of

A Footnote to History made his position in the island far easier, its obvious fairness being generally recognised.

Sidney Colvin says : " On the whole the year had been a prosperous one, full of successful work and eager interests, although darkened in its later months by disquietude on account of his wife's health. He had himself well maintained the improved strength and the renewed capacity both for literary work and outdoor activity which life in the South Seas had brought him from the first."

The Stevensons accumulated a considerable household at Vailima, and except that vegetables were almost impossible to obtain, they had little difficulty with their stores. Oranges and mangoes grew on the estate, and several acres were planted with pineapples. But the plantation never paid its way, Stevenson being far too generous an employer. Sir Graham Balfour relates that Stevenson habitually rose at six and at once began to work. Half an hour later, he had a light breakfast, and he went on working by himself until about half-past eight, when his stepdaughter, who now acted as his secretary, began to take down from dictation, and this went on until noon. Late in the evening, when the rest of the household was in bed, Stevenson often started to work again. He rode a good deal, played croquet and tennis, and piquet and other card games. This was the ordinary routine, but when Stevenson was " in a hot fit of work " he would write all day long, and there was always the preoccupation of local politics.

His house was large and spacious. A hundred people could dance in the main hall, and, so Mr. Lloyd Osbourne says, except for the rack of rifles and the half-naked servants, one might have thought oneself in a Scottish or an English house. Vailima was " a fantastic extravagance," but it was well within Stevenson's means. Mr. Lloyd Osbourne has written with an acute estimate of Stevenson's character :

" His life of feudal splendour in Samoa would have seemed twice as resplendent in the retrospect ; and in some French or Italian villa I believe he would have broken his heart to return. Samoa filled his need for the dramatic and the grandiose ; he expanded on its teeming stage, where he could hold warriors in leash, and play Richelieu to half-naked kings. He had been touched by that most consuming of all ambitions —statecraft—and there was in him, hardly realised but emerging, the spirit of a great administrator, slowly bringing order out of chaos, and finding immeasurable joy in the task." [1]

He may not always have been happy in Samoa, but (I again quote Mr. Lloyd Osbourne) " he was happier there than he could have been at any place in the world."

[1] *Catriona*, Preface, p. xiv.

There were constant visitors at Vailima—an occasional tourist, sometimes the officers from a man-of-war, constantly "strange old shell-backed guests out of every quarter of the island world, their mouths full of oaths for which they will punctiliously apologise, and their clothes unmistakably purchased in a trade room, each probably followed by a dusky bride." [1]

As his life drew to an end, it is clear that Henley was perfectly right, and that the Shorter Catechist in Stevenson became stronger and stronger. He was on intimate personal terms with the Protestant missionaries in the island, and for a time helped them in their work by taking a Bible Class on Sunday afternoons. The policy of the Catholic missionaries appealed to him. They had a far closer social connection with the people; in Sir Graham Balfour's words, "they encouraged all native habits and traditions at all compatible with Christianity, and while they were by no means indifferent to the welfare of the poor, they pleased Stevenson—he was always proclaiming himself an aristocrat—by endeavouring to obtain converts from persons of position and rank."

In 1892 Stevenson began a correspondence with J. M. Barrie, whom he had never seen. "We are both Scots," he wrote, "and I suspect both rather Scotty Scots; my own Scottishness tends to intermittency but is at times erisypelitous."

---

[1] *Life of R. L. Stevenson*, by Graham Balfour, vol. ii. p. 125.

His literary judgments in these later years of his life are extremely interesting. Despite his quarrel with Henley, he retained all his old admiration for his friend's work : " He is one of those who can make a noise of his own with words, and in whom experience strikes an individual note. There is perhaps no more genuine poet living, bar the Big Guns. In case I cannot overtake an acknowledgment to himself by this mail, please let him hear of my pleasure and admiration. How poorly Kipling compares! He is all smart journalism and cleverness : it is all bright and shallow and limpid, like a business paper—a good one, *s'entend* ; but there is no blot of heart's blood and the Old Night ; there are no harmonics, there is scarce harmony to his music ; and in Henley—all these ; a touch, a sense within sense, a sound outside sound, the shadow of the inscrutable, eloquent beyond all definition. The first *London Voluntary* knocked me wholly."

Of Zola's *Débâcle*, he wrote to Sidney Colvin : " I am now well on with the third part of the *Débâcle*. The two first I liked much ; the second completely knocking me ; so far as it has gone, this third part appears the ramblings of a dull man who has forgotten what he has to say—he reminds me of an M.P. But Sedan was really great, and I will pick no holes."

To Barrie he wrote : " *The Little Minister* ought to have ended badly ; we all know it did and we are infinitely grateful to you for the grace and good feeling with which you lied about it. If you had told the truth, I for one could never have forgiven you." Of Marion Crawford's writing he said : " It has got life to it and guts in it and it moves." And of Barrie : " Stuff in that young man, but he must see and not be too funny ; genius in him, but there is a journalist at his elbow ; there 's the risk." " I have no use for Anatole," he said in 1893. " He writes very prettily—and then afterwards." A year later he had changed his mind. " I have made the acquaintance of the *Abbé Coignard* and have become a faithful adorer. I don't think a better book was ever written." He admired the writings of Paul Bourget, and was mightily offended when the French novelist failed to acknowledge a letter of homage.

To his other literary estimates may be added a letter to Conan Doyle, written in April 1893, complimenting him on the publication of the first series of adventures of *Sherlock Holmes* : " That is the class of literature that I like when I have the toothache. As a matter of fact, it was a pleurisy I was enjoying when I took the volume up ; and it will interest you as a medical man to know that the cure was for the moment effectual. Only the one thing troubles me : can this be my old friend Joe Bell ? "

In 1893 Stevenson paid his last visit to Sydney,

where, as usual, he was very ill, and in the autumn of the year, he went to Honolulu, where he developed pneumonia, and his life was in such danger that his wife was hurriedly sent for. Once more, and for the last time, he recovered and went back with her to Vailima in November. In the preceding autumn another civil war had broken out in Samoa, which resulted in the defeat and banishment of his friend Mataafa, who, he believed, was the only native chief with any capacity for government. But the result of the war was a considerable reform in the local administration. In 1893 Stevenson finished *The Ebb Tide*, finished his family records, which were published with the title of *A Family of Engineers*, and began *St. Ives*. *The Ebb Tide*, he told Sidney Colvin, " seems to me to go off with a considerable bang ; in fact to be an extraordinary work."

But work was beginning to be very hard. " I break down at every paragraph. I observe and lie here and sweat till I can get one sentence wrung out after another." And he added : " I am discontented with *The Ebb Tide* naturally, there seems such a veil of words over it." In a letter to S. R. Crockett he wrote :

" Be it known to this fluent generation that I, R. L. S., in the forty-third year of my age and the twentieth of my professional life, wrote twenty-four pages in twenty-one days, working from six to eleven, and again in the afternoon from two to four or so, without fail or interruption.   Such are the gifts the gods have endowed us withal ; such was the facility of this prolific writer ! "

In the summer he was ill with " dyspepsia, over-smoking and unremunerative over-work." Much of his writing had to be rewritten.   There is in his diary the constant suggestion of ever-increasing weariness, and he had the growing resentment, common to all sick men, of having to give up pleasant habits.   He wrote to Henry James :

" I have had to stop all strong drink and all tobacco, and am now in a transition state between the two, which seems to be near madness. You never smoked, I think, so you can never taste the joys of stopping it.   But at least you have drunk, and you can enter perhaps into my annoyance when I suddenly find a glass of claret or a brandy-and-water giving me a splitting headache. Tobacco is just as bad for me.   If I live through this breach of habit, I shall be a white-livered puppy indeed.   Actually I am so made, or so twisted, that I do not like to think of life without the red wine on the table, and the tobacco with its lovely little coal of fire.   It doesn't amuse me from a distance.   I may find it the Garden of Eden when I go in, but I don't like the colour of the gate-posts."

In September 1893 he wrote to George Meredith the first and only letter sent to Box Hill from the Pacific Islands.   In it he said : " I am the head of a household of five whites and of twelve Samoans, to all of whom I am the chief and father : my cook comes to me and asks leave to marry—and his mother, a fine old chief woman, who has never lived here, does the same. You may be sure I granted the petition. It is a life of great interest, complicated by the Tower of Babel, that old enemy. And I have all the time on my hands for literary work." The letter concluded : " This is a devilish egotistical yarn. Will you try to imitate me in that if the spirit ever moves you to reply ? And meantime be sure that away in the midst of the Pacific there is a house on a wooded island where the name of George Meredith is very dear, and his memory (since it must be no more) is continually honoured."

Sidney Colvin disliked *The Ebb Tide*, and told Stevenson so, and in reply its author wrote :

" Life is not all Beer and Skittles. The inherent tragedy of things works itself out from white to black and blacker, and the poor things of a day look ruefully on. Does it shake my castiron faith ? I cannot say it does, I believe in an ultimate decency of things ; ay, and if I woke in hell, should still believe it ! But it is hard walking, and I can see my own share in the missteps, and can bow my head to the result, like an old, stern, unhappy devil of a Norseman, as my ultimate character is."

This letter was written in August when Stevenson was busy with *St Ives*, which he believed would not be wholly bad. On December 28th he wrote to Richard Le Gallienne : " I begin to grow old. I have given my top note, I fancy, and I have written too many books." In the same month he told Sidney Colvin : " I have to announce that I am off work, probably for six months. I must own that I have overworked bitterly—there, that 's legible. My hand is a thing that was, and in the meanwhile so are my brains."

In 1894, the last year of his life, Stevenson was vastly heartened by the news of the publication of the Edinburgh edition of his writings, an enterprise due to the loyalty of his old friend, Charles Baxter, and the success of which meant the removal, for a time at least, of financial anxiety. He was heartened by the growing affection shown to him by the people of the island, who remade the road leading to his house and christened it the Road of Loving Hearts. Though he worked with difficulty, he added chapters to *St. Ives* and *Weir of Hermiston*. In April he wrote a charming letter to W. B. Yeats, after reading his *Lake Isle of Innisfree* : " It is so quaint and airy, simple, artful, and eloquent to the heart." And in the collected letters, after an interval of years, there is in April 1894 a particularly attractive letter to Mrs. Sitwell, enclosing a photograph of Tusitala :

" I shall never do a better book than *Catriona*,

that is my high-water mark, and the trouble of
production increases on me at a great rate—and
mighty anxious about how I am to leave my
family : an elderly man, with elderly pre-occu-
pations, whom I should be ashamed to show you
for your old friend ; but not a hope of my dying
soon and cleanly, and ' winning off the stave.'
Rather I am daily better in physical health. I
shall have to see this business out, after all ; and
I think, in that case, they should have—they
might have—spared me all my ill-health this
decade past, if it were not to unbar the doors. I
have no taste for old age, and my nose is to be
rubbed in it in spite of my face. I was meant to
die young, and the gods do not love me."

His judgment of *Catriona* was shared by Henry
James, who wrote : " *Catriona* so reeks and hums
with genius that there is no refuge for the desperate reader but in straightforward prostration."

In his correspondence, indication follows indication that he feels his race is nearly run and his
work nearly done. "My work goes along slowly,"
he said to his cousin. " I have got to a crossing
place, I suppose ; the present book, *St. Ives*, is
nothing ; it is in no style in particular, a tissue
of adventures, the central character not very
well done, no philosophic pith under the yarn ;
and, in short, if people will read it, that 's all I
ask ; and if they won't, damn them ! "

In October he wrote to Sidney Colvin : " I do

not think my health can be so hugely improved,
without some subsequent improvement in my
brains. Though, of course, there is the possi-
bility that literature is a morbid secretion, and
abhors health ! I do not think it is possible to
have fewer illusions than I. I sometimes wish
I had more. They are amusing. But I cannot
take myself seriously, as an artist ; the limitations are so obvious. I did take myself seriously as a workman of old, but my practice has
fallen off. I am now an idler and cumberer of
the ground ; it may be excused to me perhaps
by twenty years of industry and ill-health, which
have taken the cream off the milk."

And in the last letter that he wrote to the same
constant correspondent : " O it is bad to grow
old. For me it is practically hell. I do not like
the consolations of age. I was born a young
man ; I have continued so ; and before I end, a
pantaloon, a driveller."

Two days before his death he wrote to Gosse
thanking him for the dedication in the volume of
his poems *In Russet and Silver* : " It is beautifully
said, beautifully and kindly felt ; and I should be
a churl indeed if I were not grateful, and an ass
if I were not proud. I remember when Symonds
dedicated a book to me ; I wrote and told him of
' the pang of gratified vanity ' with which I had
read it. The pang was present again, but how
much more sober and autumnal — like your

volume." The letter concludes : " May you live
long, since it seems as if you would continue to
enjoy life. May you write many more books as
good as this one—only there 's one thing impossible, you can write never another dedication
that can give the same pleasure to the vanished
TUSITALA."

In the course of the dedication, Sir Edmund
Gosse says :

> By strange pathways God hath brought you,
>   Tusitala,
> In strange webs of fortune caught you,
> Led you by strange moods and measures
> To this paradise of pleasures !
> And the body-guard that sought you
> To conduct you home to glory,—
> Dark the oriflammes carried,
> In the mist their cohort tarried,—
> They were Languor, Pain, and Sorrow,
>   Tusitala ! [1]

On the afternoon of December 3rd, 1894,
Stevenson took his morning work, the last chapters he ever wrote of *Weir of Hermiston,* to his wife
for her criticism. Mrs. Sanchez says in her biography of her sister : " She quickly perceived
that in this, which neither dreamed was to be
the last work of his pen, his genius had risen to its
highest level, and she poured out her praise in a
way that was unusual with her. It was almost
with her words of commendation still ringing in

[1] *In Russet and Silver,* by Edmund Gosse, p. xi.

his ears that he passed to the great beyond." [1]
No woman was ever a sounder critic of her husband's work. When Henley read *Weir of Hermiston*, he wrote : " I 've found my Lewis again and in all his glory," and Mr. Chesterton has said that in *Weir of Hermiston* there are " richer shades of passion than he had ever yet attempted to touch."

Stevenson's last hours have been described by Mr. Lloyd Osbourne : " He said he was hungry ; begged her assistance to help him make a salad for the evening meal ; and to enhance the little feast he brought up a bottle of old Burgundy from the cellar. He was helping his wife on the verandah, and gaily talking, when suddenly he put both his hands to his head and cried out : ' What 's that ? ' Then he asked quickly : ' Do I look strange ? ' Even as he did so, he fell on his knees beside her. Just as he had leaned upon her for help, comfort, and advice for so many years of his life, so it was at her feet that he sank in death when the last swift summons came. He was helped into the great hall, between his wife and his body-servant, Sosimo, and at ten minutes past eight, the same evening, Monday, December 3, 1894, he passed away."

" It is I who should go, not he, who is young and loved," George Meredith wrote when he heard of his death, and in his *Stevenson*, Mr.

---

[1] *Life of Mrs. R. L. Stevenson*, by N. V. de G. Sanchez, p. 220.

Chesterton says: "I was a lad when the news came to England; and I remember that some of his friends doubted at first, because the telegram said that he died making a salad; and they 'had never heard of his doing such a thing.' And I remember fancying, with a secret arrogance, that I knew one thing about him better than they did, though I never saw him with these mortal eyes; for it seemed to me that if there were something that Stevenson had never been known to do before, it would be the very thing that he would do. So indeed he died mixing new salads of many sorts." [1]

The Union Jack had always flown over the house at Vailima. When he died, the flag was hauled down and placed over his body, which was watched through the night by his Samoan retainers. Chief after chief came to pay tribute of love and affection, and the Prayers for the Dead were recited by the native Roman Catholics. A path up the steep face of the mountain was cut by willing labour, and the grave was dug at the summit.

Was ever man buried in a more beautiful place. In his recently published *Samoa Under the Sailing Gods*, Mr. N. A. Rowe says:

"The top of the mountain is flat, like a table, and turf-covered; no bigger than the floor of a room. Between a break in the trees, Apia Road-

---

[1] *Stevenson*, by G. K. Chesterton, p. 181.

stead can be seen, far below and very tiny, with the water in the bay a concentrated blue, and that upon the reef white and creamy, its noise amounting here only to a gentle murmur, and the expanse of empty ocean that slants upwards to the sky seems vast indeed. At the edge of the arborial frame, I remember, on the occasion of my visit, was a scarlet-blossomed tree—not an hibiscus—in flower, and the birds all about were singing and twittering like an English spring ; for, as in Australia, the songless birds and the scentless flowers, are here a myth."

At one o'clock on December 5th the body, still covered by the British flag, was carried up the rocky path. Nineteen Europeans and sixty Samoans were Stevenson's mourners, and included in the funeral service was one of the prayers that Stevenson had written at Vailima, and which he had read to the family for the first time on the night before his death :

" We beseech Thee, Lord, to behold us with favour, folk of many families and nations, gathered together in the peace of this roof; weak men and women, subsisting under the covert of Thy patience. Be patient still ; suffer us yet a while longer—with our broken purposes of good, with our idle endeavours against evil, suffer us a while longer to endure, and (if it may be) help us to do better. Bless to us our extraordinary mercies ; if the day come when these must be taken, have us play the man under affliction. Be with our friends ; be with ourselves. Go with each of us to rest ; if any awake, temper to them the dark hours of watching ; and when the day returns to us, our sun and comforter, call us up with morning faces and with morning hearts—eager to labour—eager to be happy, if happiness shall be our portion—and if the day be marked for sorrow, strong to endure it. We thank Thee and praise Thee ; and in the words of Him to whom this day is sacred, close our oblation." [1]

Over his grave was written the Requiem which he had composed years before.

Sir Arthur Quiller-Couch says in his essay on the *Death of R. L. Stevenson* : " For the good of man, his father and grandfather planted the high sea-lights upon the Inchcape and the Tyree Coast. He, the last of their line, nursed another light and tended it. Their lamps still shine upon the Bell Rock and the Skerryvore ; and—though in alien seas, upon a rock of exile—this other light shall continue, unquenchable by age, beneficent, serene." [2]

[1] *Letters*, vol. v., Appendix I., p. 189.
[2] *Modern English Essays*, vol. iii. p. 190.

CHAPTER XI

THE LITERARY ARTIST

IN his article on Stevenson in the *Encyclopaedia Britannica*, Sir Edmund Gosse said : " He was always assiduously graceful, always desiring to present his idea, his image, his rhapsody, in as persuasive a light as possible, and, particularly, with as much harmony as possible. He had mastered his manner, and one may say, learned his trade, in the exercise of criticism and the reflective parts of literature, before he surrendered himself to that powerful creative impulse which had long been tempting him, so that when, in mature life, he essayed the portraiture of invented character he came to it unhampered by any imperfection of language."

Stevenson wrote at a time when style was generally disregarded by English writers. As a matter of fact, of sad fact maybe, a good novel may be very badly written. Professor George Saintsbury has said :

" It is a pity that a novel should not be well written : yet some of the greatest novels of the world are, as no one of the greatest poems of the world is, or could possibly be, written anything but well. It is, at any rate, rather annoying that the plot of a novel should hang loosely together, that the chronology should be obviously impossible, that the author should forget on page 200 what page 100 has told his readers, that there should be little beginning, less middle, and no end. Yet some of the great, some of the greatest novels of the world, are open to objections of this kind." [1] Stevenson was never guilty of these blunderings.

In her brilliant study of Henry James, Miss Rebecca West says that " style was poisoned at the fount of thought by Carlyle whose sentences were confused disasters like railway accidents, and by Herbert Spencer, who wrote as though he were the offspring of two *Times* leaders." [2] Stevenson himself said in a letter to Richard Le Gallienne that the British public love " the styleless, the shapeless, the slap-dash and the disorderly." Almost alone among the novelists of his time, he loved words and phrases for their own sake. The late Lord Rosebery once said : " Mr. Fox said of Mr. Pitt that he himself (Mr. Fox) had always a command of words, but that Mr. Pitt had always a command of the right words, and that is the quality which strikes us in the style of Stevenson." [3]

[1] *Collected Essays and Papers* (Saintsbury), vol. iii. p. 142.
[2] *Henry James*, by Rebecca West, p. 81.
[3] *More Books on the Table*, by Edmund Gosse, p. 272.

An acute French critic, M. Louis Cazamian, has written : " Stevenson devoted very attentive care to the art of writing. He knew the anxious quest of the exact word, the search for a cadence at the same time harmonious and not too markedly regular. His style is sufficiently nervous to bear such conscious filing and refining. It draws its strength from a very varied and simple vocabulary, in which the whole scale of learned shades meets with the most racy vein—popular, technical or dialectal words. At times the exquisiteness of the form seems to exceed the just demands of the matter, and this is the single weakness of that prose." [1]   And Sir Arthur Conan Doyle has written : " The main characteristic of Stevenson is his curious instinct for saying in the briefest space just those few words which stamp the impression upon the reader's mind." [2]

After the publication of *Catriona*, Henry James wrote to him : " It has been long before that since any decent sentence was turned in English." Professor Saintsbury has said that Stevenson had " a true hold on the romantic," and has suggested that he suffered from living in a literary age and from his eager desire to arrive at perfect expression.

" Mr. Stevenson presents for us, in a new and

---

[1] *A History of English Literature*, by Émile Legouis and Louis Cazamian, vol. ii. p. 440.

[2] *Through the Magic Door*, by Conan Doyle, p. 245.

extremely interesting form, the problem whether
it would not have been better for him to have been
born in a period not ' literary ' at all.   In such a
case he might have written nothing ; but in such
a case, had he written anything, his native fund
of humour and of imagination, his hardly sur-
passed faculty of telling a story (though not
exactly of finishing one), his wit, his command at
once of the pathetic and the horrible, must have
found organs of expression which would not have
been choked and chained and distorted as they
were by the effort to imitate—to make a style
eclectic yet original.   But we may very well be
thankful for him as he was, and hope that the
first great novelist of the coming century will be
half as good as he, the last exclusively of the
nineteenth." [1]

Stevenson had—I quote Walter Raleigh—" a
fine sense, in the first place, of the sound, value,
meaning and associations of individual words, and
next a sense of harmony, proportion and effect
in their combinations."   Raleigh admits that " it
is amazing what a nobility a mere truism is often
found to possess when it is clad with a garment
thus woven."   Truisms indeed abound in Stevenson's essays.   " Mankind was never so happily
inspired as when it made a cathedral," he wrote
in *An Inland Voyage*.   A truism indeed, said by a
thousand men before.   But Stevenson goes on to

[1] *A Short History of English Literature* (Saintsbury), p. 757.

ornament the truism. A cathedral is " a thing as single and spacious as a statue to the first glance, and yet, on examination, as lively and interesting as a forest in detail." " A happy man or woman is a better thing to find than a five-pound note," is a sufficiently obvious truism. But Stevenson can even give it nobility : " their entrance into a room is as though another candle had been lighted."

Mr. H. G. Wells said in a letter to Henry James: " To you literature like painting is an end. To me literature like architecture is a means. It has a use." To an extent Stevenson would have agreed with Mr. Wells. He was a moralist with the itch to preach. He became a teller of tales. Always for him literature was a means, and generally Sir Edmund Gosse is justified in the assertion that Stevenson kept his love of words " within the bounds of good sense and literary decorum." Sir Edmund suggests that the letters and essays— " those exquisite mixtures of wisdom, pathos, and humour "—are Stevenson's most important contribution to literature. Certainly the mixture was achieved with the greatest care. In his essay *On Some Technical Elements of Style in Literature*, Stevenson said that writers have two tasks, " the task of artfully combining the prime elements of language into phrases that shall be musical in the mouth ; the task of weaving their argument into a texture of committed phrases and of rounded

periods." And in *Lay Morals* Stevenson says :
" Every piece of work which is not as good as
you can make it, which you have palmed off
imperfect, meagrely thought, niggardly in execution, upon mankind, who is your paymaster on
parole, and in a sense your pupil, every hasty or
slovenly or untrue performance, should rise up
against you in the court of your own heart and
condemn you for a thief."

The performance must be meticulously careful.
That is a point of honour. The author owes it
to the reader that his writing shall be as perfect
as possible, and the author must be even more
interested and obsessed with his medium, with,
that is, the manner of telling, than with the
tale that is told. In the essay on *Fontainebleau*,
Stevenson says : " The love of words and not
a desire to publish new discoveries, the love
of form and not a novel reading of historical
events, mark the vocation of the writer and the
painter."

The love of words and the strain to find the
right word unquestionably involve the danger of
strain and artificiality. In his essay on Shelley,
Francis Thompson says : " Theoretically, of
course, one ought always to try for the best word.
But practically, the habit of excessive care in
word-selection frequently results in loss of spontaneity ; and, still worse, the habit of always
taking the most ornate word, the word most

removed from ordinary speech." [1] No one will
deny that there is sometimes over-strain in Stevenson's writings. Walter Raleigh admits that " his
careful choice of epithet and name have even been
criticised as lending to some of his narrative writing an excessive air of deliberation." In his review of Sir Graham Balfour's *Life*, Henley says
that Stevenson's style " is so perfectly achieved
that the achievement gets obvious ; and when
achievement gets obvious, is it not by way of becoming uninteresting ? " Mr. Benson considers
that Stevenson had, in Francis Thompson's words,
an excessive love for the most ornate word, while
admitting that his style at its best is " graceful and
picturesque." He adds that " at its worst it is
sheer journalism, pretentious and stilted, and it is
always his master, not his servant. It compelled
him, as under the lash, to sacrifice simplicity to
the desire to be striking and sonorous, and to
arrest attention for what is trivial by some unusual phrase, just as he called attention to himself by outlandish habiliments. . . . In this craze
for picturesque phrasing, Stevenson decks his
scullions and beachcombers with jewels of speech
that sit ludicrously on their aprons and rags. He
commits in fact the error of making his characters
talk in the style he has hewn out for himself."
How far is this criticism justified ? I take two
passages almost at hazard. First from *Treasure*

[1] *Old Style*, by Sir Arthur Quiller-Couch, p. 208.

Island, when John Silver is persuading one of the crew of the *Hispaniola* to join the mutineers :

" Gentlemen of fortune," returned the cook, " usually trusts little among themselves, and right they are, you may lay to it. But I have a way with me, I have. When a mate brings a slip on his cable—one as knows me, I mean—it won't be in the same world with old John. There was some that was feared of Pew, and some that was feared of Flint ; but Flint his own self was feared of me. Feared he was, and proud. They was the roughest crew afloat, was Flint's ; the devil himself would have been feared to go to sea with them. Well, now, I tell you, I 'm not a boasting man, and you seen yourself how easy I keep company ; but when I was quartermaster, *lambs* wasn't the word for Flint's old Buccaneers. Ah, you may be sure of yourself in old John's ship."

" Well, I tell you now," replied the lad, " I didn't half a quarter like the job till I had this talk with you, John ; but there 's my hand on it now."

That was written at the beginning of Stevenson's career as a novelist. My second quotation is taken from *The Ebb Tide,* written at the end of his career as a novelist :

" Huish means the same as what I do," said Davis. " When that man came stepping around, and saying, ' Look here, I 'm Attwater '—and you knew it was so, by God !—I sized him right straight up. Here 's the real article, I said, and I don't like it ; here 's the real first-rate copper-bottomed aristocrat. ' *Aw! don't know ye, do I ? God damn ye, did God make ye ? '* No, that couldn't be nothing but genuine ; a man got to be born to that, and notice ! smart as champagne and hard as nails ; no kind of a fool ; no, *sir !* not a pound of him ! Well, what 's he here upon this beastly island for ? I said. *He 's* not here collecting eggs. He 's a palace at home, and powdered flunkies ; and if he don't stay there, you bet he knows the reason why ! Follow ? "

" O yes, I 'ear you," said Huish.

" He 's been doing good business here, then," continued the captain. " For ten years, he 's been doing a great business. It 's pearl and shell, of course ; there couldn't be nothing else in such a place, and no doubt the shell goes off regularly by this *Trinity Hall,* and the money for it straight into the bank, so that 's no use to us. But what else is there ? Is there nothing else he would be likely to keep here ? Is there nothing else he would be bound to keep here ? Yes, sir ; the pearls ! First, because they 're too valuable to trust out of his hands. Second, because pearls want a lot of handling and matching ; and the man who sells his pearls as they come in, one here, one there, instead of hanging back and holding up—well, that man 's a fool, and it 's not Attwater."

" Likely," said Huish, " that 's w'at it is ; not proved, but likely."

" It 's proved," said Davis bluntly.

" Suppose it was ? " said Herrick. " Suppose that was all so, and he had these pearls—a ten years' collection of them ?—Suppose he had ? There 's my question."

Can it be fairly said that Stevenson makes his characters talk in the style he has hewn out for

himself ? On the contrary, it is abundantly clear
from these two extracts that he makes his characters speak in their manner as they live.

Stevenson was a " sedulous " workman. He
had carefully learned his art. He was no im-
provisator. He was in fact a master craftsman,
and his craft was the handling of the English
language. Walter Raleigh says that his teachers
were " the most vigorous of the prose writers of
the seventeenth and early eighteenth centuries."
But it was to Hazlitt and to Lamb that he
played " the sedulous ape." Possibly, as Henley
suggested, he never wrote as well as either,
but they were his models. Doubtless, too, he
owed something to Sterne. Sir Edmund Gosse
says : " I am not sure that of all the books
which Stevenson read, it was not the *Sentimental
Journey* which made the deepest impression upon
him." [1]

The only contemporary writer, apart, perhaps,
from Henley, whom Stevenson can be said in any
sense to have imitated, is George Meredith. The
influence is evident in *Prince Otto*. In his *Through
the Magic Door*, Sir Arthur Conan Doyle says :
" Stevenson was deeply influenced by Meredith,
and even in these books (*Treasure Island* and *The
Black Arrow*) the influence of the master is apparent. There is the apt use of an occasional
archaic or unusual word, the short strong de-

[1] *Some Diversions of a Man of Letters*, by Edmund Gosse, p. 100.

R

scriptions, the striking metaphors, the somewhat staccato fashion of speech." [1]

Professor Sarolea has written a whole book on the debt that Stevenson owed to France and of his affinity with the French genius. Like all conscious stylists, Stevenson was, of course, a disciple of Flaubert, and Professor Sarolea says :

" All critics are agreed that the originality of Stevenson consists mainly in the unique quality of his style. And my contention is that it is the loving and minute study of French models at an early age under the blue skies of the Riviera which has made him a master of style. It is rank heresy to imagine that the stylist is born not made. Perfection of form is generally the outcome of a long and painstaking training. That is the explanation of Stevenson's countless abortive attempts. No writer has left so many unfinished books." [2]

Professor Saintsbury has written : " Of the four most remarkable men of letters of my own generation whom I knew most intimately, and who now navigate ' the unequal waters of the dead,' one could find parallels for three. Stevenson was a sort of Maturin-Borrow, with a better temperament and a higher sense of art than either ; Henley was a minor Johnson, a little damaged in some parts ; Traill, the strongest of all, was a Swift who too often bound if not blinded himself

[1] *Through the Magic Door*, by Conan Doyle, p. 241.
[2] *R. L. Stevenson and France* (Sarolea), p. 53.

at the mill with slaves. But Lang was only and always Lang ; even the Thackerayan touches in him kept their own and his own nature." [1]

Maturin-Borrow is a very suggestive combination. Maturin was an Irish writer, now entirely forgotten, who wrote a thriller, famous in its day, *Melmoth the Wanderer*. And Professor Saintsbury's astute comparison of Stevenson with Borrow strengthens my suggestion that he was always the Shorter Catechist. But from whomsoever he learned and whomsoever he made his models, Stevenson's style was his own, and, as always in writers of genius, and even in writers of talent, the style was the man. " The style can never be separated from the man," said Sir Arthur Quiller-Couch in his Cambridge Lectures on *The Art of Writing*, and in a finely suggestive phrase, Walter Raleigh describes style as " the index of persons." The man revealed in the writing of Stevenson is, without question, immensely attractive. Newman says that a gentleman is " simple as he is forcible, and as brief as he is decisive." Accepting this definition, the Stevenson of the Essays, the Letters, and the Novels is most decidedly a gentleman.

Mr. Benson declares that Stevenson was always trying for effect, that he sacrificed simplicity to the desire to be striking, that he was the slave of the picturesque phrase. If this were true, it

[1] *A Scrap Book* (Saintsbury), p. 68.

would be the condemnation of Stevenson as a literary artist, for there can be no quarrel with Sir Arthur Quiller-Couch's assertion that " art's truest maxim is to avoid excess," a maxim that pillories Carlyle.

I do not find this true of Stevenson. He had quite properly a great concern for emphasis and, indeed, in no modern writer is meaning conveyed more successfully by judicious emphasis. But with his emphasis he rarely indulges in mere rhetoric and, as it seems to me, far from letting his love of words run away with him, he holds himself well in hand, using his style as a servant to achieve the end which he had in mind.

It is possible, of course, to find Stevenson or bits of Stevenson in many of his characters, but by no means to the same extent as Mr. Wells and bits of Mr. Wells are to be found in Mr. Lewisham, in Kipps, in Mr. Polly, in Mr. Britling, and in William Clissold ; or as Mr. Bernard Shaw is to be found in most of the heroines of his plays, not excluding *Saint Joan*. In the creation of his characters, indeed, he has carried out Flaubert's maxim, " You should by an intellectual effort transport yourself into characters, not draw them into yourself." All his characters, or perhaps it would be safer to say, nearly all of them, have a convincing reality. It is indeed the triumph of *Treasure Island* and the quality that differentiates it from the ordinary adventure story, beloved by boys, that the characters are real, that the reader is convinced that he would be terrified to death if he were brought face to face with blind Pew or with Long John Silver or with Israel Hands.

No fictional characters ever live unless they are convincingly real. Henry James says that " the reality of Don Quixote and Mr. Micawber is of a very delicate shade." But whatever the delicacy of the shade, there is the magnificent reality. No man, indeed, can possibly live long in the world, if he have eyes to see and a heart to understand, without meeting Don Quixote, perhaps with his magnificence modified, and Mr. Micawber, perhaps with his volubility checked and his optimism chastened. So it is with the characters of Stevenson. Who can doubt the reality of Long John Silver or of Pew, that awesome blind man, or of Israel Hands ? Who has not met a Prince Otto, with his easy philosophy—" What matters it how bad we are, if others can still love us and we can still love others ? " Mrs. Stevenson says that Prince Otto was modelled on Stevenson's cousin Robert, and that before the novel was finished, Stevenson was convinced that Prince Otto was himself. But whoever he may resemble, he is genuine flesh and blood, and however unsatisfactory his philosophy may be, it is in accord with human experience. What man was ever loved for stern virtue ? It is generally our little failings that secure friendship for us. And if Prince Otto is a human if unheroic hero, what a very real villain is Huish, whose mixture of savage brutality and courage mark him as the forerunner of the Chicago gangster.

It has been frequently said of Stevenson that he was unable to create women characters. The Shorter Catechist either acquires the harem habit, as John Knox acquired it, or grows fearful of women as the inviters to iniquity. I have already said that the naughtiness of Stevenson, both in Edinburgh and Paris, has been absurdly exaggerated. And whatever may have been his sex adventures, they came to an end with his singularly lucky marriage. Afterwards, but for his wife, it was men who alone interested him. The theme of his novels was adventure, masculine adventure. It would have been as ridiculously inartistic to have dragged a " love interest " into *Treasure Island* as it was when its author dragged a " love interest " into *Looking Backward*, the Socialist novel of my boyhood. And while Stevenson could describe a Huish, with understanding and a certain measure of sympathy, his finicky Puritan soul would have revolted against the sort of woman that Huish would have loved, probably only for a night, certainly not for a lifetime. Perhaps, too, like David Balfour, " he was much in fear of mocking from the womenkind."

The few women in his novels are clear-cut and real, and it is interesting that all, or nearly all, of them are Scotswomen, from Catriona—" she had wonderful bright eyes like stars "—to Flora Gilchrist in *St. Ives*, with her " air of angelic candour, yet of a high spirit." Of all the women of the Stevenson novels, the elder Kirstie in *Weir of Hermiston* (was she suggested by " Cummy " ?) is the most attractive : " Kirstie was now over fifty, and might have sat to a sculptor. Long of limb, and still light of foot, deep-breasted, robust-loined, her golden hair not yet mingled with any trace of silver, the years had but caressed and embellished her. By the lines of a rich and vigorous maternity, she seemed destined to be the bride of heroes and the mother of their children."

Miss Masson has well described Stevenson's women — " young women and old women, Highland and Lowland,—but all Scotswomen ; the women of his memory, the women of his youth."

In the choice of his plots, Stevenson was primarily influenced by his own predilections, and only secondarily by consideration for the audience to whom he was appealing.

In his lectures on the *Psychology of Style*, Mr. Middleton Murry writes that if an author has to get his living by his work, " he will have to take into account the taste of the age. If it is an active and enthusiastic age, he will to some extent be in sympathy with its taste. He will be able to choose a plot which may not be all that he would desire in point of delicacy and subtlety, but lends itself to the bent of his own mode of experience, his emotional predisposition." [1] Stevenson began to write novels to please a boy, but incidentally he wrote *Treasure Island* to please himself quite as much as to please young Lloyd Osbourne. He wrote *Kidnapped* partly because he was a Scotsman and partly because he was fascinated by the character of Alan Breck. The South Sea stories emerged naturally from his keen interest in the beachcombers with whom he had drunk and gossiped. His plots and his characters, that is to say, grew naturally out of his own character, his own heredity, and his own experience, exactly as the plots and characters of Dickens grew out of his character, his heredity, and his experience. He told the tales that he had to tell, the tales that no other man could have told, and he told his tales in his own peculiar manner, a manner which no other man could have exactly reproduced.

No man who lived as lustily as Stevenson lived could possibly have become a mere stylist writing for the joy of writing and for nothing else. The fact of his famous and friendly controversy with Henry James impels a comparison between the two men. Mr. Middleton Murry says of Henry James : " With the decline of his power of receiving a direct emotional impulse from the life he desired to represent, he transferred the object of

---

[1] *The Problem of Style*, by Middleton Murry, p. 30.

his interest to the process of representation. This is a danger that always threatens the extremely conscious literary artist, and it is the more insidious because it is fascinating. Technique begins to assume a life of its own ; it is graced by complications, subtleties, and economies which dance inextricable patterns in the void ; the work of the novelist slips free of the control of verisimilitude, and, insensibly, he resigns the peculiar privilege of the creative artist, the arduous joy of compelling words to accept a strange content and a new significance, for the subtle but sterile satisfaction of contemplating them as they revolve in obedience to their own law." [1] Miss Rebecca West says that Henry James's phrases compelled his characters " to do things which they never did. For the metaphors are so beautiful and completely presented to the mind that it retains them as having as real and physical an existence as the facts." [2] Henry James was the veritable slave of words. Stevenson never was a slave of words, though he might well have been had he not become, by the grace of God, a writer of novels of adventure, or if he had not himself been born an adventurer, who would have thoroughly enjoyed sailing for Treasure Island under the Jolly Roger.

" It will be found true, I believe," he said, " in a

---

[1] *The Problem of Style*, by Middleton Murry, pp. 21, 22.
[2] *Henry James*, by Rebecca West, p. 112.

majority of cases that the artist writes with more
gusto and effect of those things which he has only
wished to do than of those which he has done.
Desire is a wonderful telescope and Pisgah the
best observatory." [1]

Walter Besant declared that a novel must consist of adventures. Henry James retorted that it
is as absurd to say that fiction cannot exist without adventure as to say that it can exist without
" matrimony, or celibacy, or parturition, or
cholera, or hydropathy, or Jansenism ! " [2]   To
Henry James, fiction is " an immense and exquisite correspondence with life." Nothing in
the life of a man is outside the scope of the novelist.
Mr. H. G. Wells has expressed this in a different
way :

" We are going to write, subject only to our
own limitations, about the whole of human life.
We are going to deal with political questions and
social questions. We cannot present people unless we have this free hand, this unrestricted field.
What is the good of telling stories about people's
lives if one may not deal freely with the religious
beliefs and organisations that have controlled or
failed to control them ?

" What is the good of pretending to write about
love and the loyalties and treacheries and quarrels
of men and women if one must not glance at those

[1] *The Writer's Art*, by R. W. Brown, p. 239.
[2] *Ibid.*, p. 225.

varieties of physical temperament and organic quality, those deeply passionate needs and distresses from which half the storms of human life are brewed ? We are going to write about it all. We are going to write about business and finance and politics and precedents and pretentiousness and decorum and indecorum until a thousand pretences and ten thousand impostors shrivel in the cold clear air of our elucidations."

But in order to carry out his ambition, Mr. Wells has been compelled to provide his characters with adventure. Both Mr. Kipps and Mr. Polly are adventurers, and even Mr. Clissold, though of him it must be admitted that his words speak louder than his actions.

Stevenson clearly differentiated between the novel of character in which the incidents are, to use his own word, " tributary," and the novel of adventure. " Danger is the matter with which this class of novel deals ; fear the passion with which it idly trifles ; and the characters are portrayed only so far as they realise the sense of danger and provoke the sympathy of fear." He imagines himself giving this advice to a young writer :

" The best that we can say to him is this : Let him choose a motive, whether of character or passion ; carefully construct his plot so that every incident is an illustration of the motive, and every property employed shall bear to it a near relation of congruity or contrast ; avoid a sub-plot, unless, as sometimes in Shakespeare, the sub-plot be a reversion or complement of the main intrigue ; suffer not his style to flag below the level of the argument ; pitch the key of conversation, not with any thought of how men talk in parlours, but with a single eye to the degree of passion he may be called on to express ; and allow neither himself in the narrative, nor any character in the course of the dialogue, to utter one sentence that is not part and parcel of the business of the story or the discussion of the problem involved. Let him not regret if this shortens his book ; it will be better so ; for to add irrevelant matter is not to lengthen but to bury. Let him not mind if he miss a thousand qualities, so that he keeps unflaggingly in pursuit of the one he has chosen. Let him not care particularly if he miss the tone of conversation, the pungent material detail of the day's manners, the reproduction of the atmosphere and the environment. These elements are not essential : a novel may be excellent, and yet have none of them ; a passion or a character is so much the better depicted as it rises clearer from material circumstance."

Here is the ideal of a conscious artist, written when fame had already come to him. Here is the master recipe of his novels. And his achievement is to be estimated by the manner in which it carried out his plan. Sir Arthur Conan Doyle says that Stevenson's novels " have pictured only one side of life, and that a strange exceptional one." To this it may be said that though his scenes are set in strange places and his characters generally live in the atmosphere of danger and fear, their emotions are always human, and the reader is forced to admit that in similar circumstances, had he possessed the qualities of the Stevenson characters, he would have acted in a similar way. That is to say, fiction, when it is the work of an artist and an observer, is as true as fact.

I quote as an example of what I mean the passage in *The Ebb Tide*, in which Stevenson describes how Herrick tried, in a fit of shame, to drown himself—and failed. As he swam he brooded on his degradation :

" From such flights of fancy, he was aroused by the growing coldness of the water. Why should he delay ? Here, where he was now, let him drop the curtain, let him seek the ineffable refuge, let him lie down with all races and generations of men in the house of sleep. It was easy to say, easy to do. To stop swimming : there was no mystery in that, if he could do it. Could he ? And he could not. He knew it instantly. He was aware instantly of an opposition in his members, unanimous and invincible, clinging to life with a single fixed resolve, finger by finger, sinew by sinew ; something that was at once he and not he—at once within and without him ; the shutting of some miniature valve in his brain, which a single manly thought should suffice to open—and the grasp of an external fate ineluct able as gravity. To any man there may come at times a consciousness that there blows, through all the articulations of his body, the wind of a spirit not wholly his ; that his mind rebels ; that another girds him and carries him whither he would not. It came now to Herrick, with the authority of a revelation. There was no escape possible. The open door was closed in his recreant face. He must go back into the world and amongst men without illusion. He must stagger on to the end with the pack of his responsibility and his disgrace, until a cold, a blow, a merciful chance ball, or the more merciful hangman, should dismiss him from his infamy. There were men who would commit suicide ; there were men who could not ; and he was one who could not."

This might be described as a perfect example of descriptive reporting. It is the completely understanding report of a man's experience.

Stevenson cared immensely for style, but it was the matter which was of the first importance to him. " *L'art de bien dire,*" he once wrote, " is but a drawing-room accomplishment, unless it be pressed into the service of truth." With some few exceptions, and those for the most part writers of small account, style to the stylist is as literature is to Mr. Wells, a means to an end. Hazlitt says in his essay *On the Difference between Writing and Speaking* :

" Words occur to him only as tallies to certain modifications of feeling. They are links in the chain of thought. His imagination is fastidious, and rejects all those that are ' of no mark or likelihood.' Certain words are in his mind indissolubly wedded to certain things ; and none are admitted at the levee of his thoughts but those of which the banns have been solemnised with scrupulous propriety."

In other words, style means the most effective method of speaking the truth, of saying what is in the writer's mind.

Writing of his contemporaries of forty years ago, Professor Saintsbury says : " When we rejoiced in them because they had followed art for art's sake, it was also, or rather at the same time, because they had followed life for life's sake *as well.* In fact you cannot do the first without doing the second, though you certainly may do the second without doing the first." [1]

It has become a truism of criticism that the most considerable work of Stevenson as a novelist is to be found in the Scottish novels, most notably in *The Master of Ballantrae* and in *Weir of Hermiston.* It is a mere personal preference, due prob-

[1] *A Scrap Book* (Saintsbury), p. 116.

ably to the fact that I am an Englishman, always rather irritated by the vernacular of the kailyard, but I infinitely prefer *Treasure Island* and the South Sea stories. So far as the Scottish stories are concerned, comparisons with Scott are inevitable, and here M. Louis Cazamian has written very wisely :

" The Scottish novels are very different from those of Sir Walter Scott ; much more modern as they are and technically conscious, much more sparing in their method, they do not show the prodigious abundance, the careless creation of unforgettable characters, which remain the birthright of the master ; still, in many respects, they bear being compared with them. Stevenson, like Scott, was steeped in the intimate knowledge of the manners and the people of Scotland ; his landscapes, more intense, reap the benefit of the gradual inurement through which, in the course of the century, the wild and grand aspects of nature had been divested of the last remnants of their repulsive horror, and had become the familiar companions of the human mind. The structure of those novels, or their liveliness, is not everywhere equal, and does not hide the weaker moments of an undermined vitality. The last, *Weir of Hermiston*, which was left unfinished, is by far the most concentrated, and promised to be a masterpiece." [1]

[1] *A History of English Literature*, by Émile Legouis and Louis Cazamian, pp. 439-40.

To this I would add that there is a far greater
dignity in Scott's characters than in most of
Stevenson's, and Stevenson—as Mr. Chesterton
has noted—has a sneaking admiration for mere
brute strength that Scott certainly never felt
or expressed.

Incidentally it may be noted that it is in craftsmanship and craftsmanship only that Stevenson
can be regarded as the pupil either of Hazlitt or
of Lamb.   His attitude to life was entirely different.   Compare, for example, Lamb's essay on *A
Complaint of the Decay of Beggars* with Stevenson's
essay on beggars in the volume *Virginibus Puerisque*.
To Lamb, with his Cockney humour, and his
Cockney conviction that all men are lovable, and
the lowest most of all, the beggar was a man and
a brother to be loved and not condemned for his
vices.   He wrote :

" Shut not thy purse-strings always against
painted distress.   Act a charity sometimes.   When
a poor creature (outwardly and visibly such)
comes before thee, do not stay to inquire whether
the ' seven small children,' in whose name he im-
plores thy assistance, have a veritable existence.
Rake not into the bowels of unwelcome truth to
save a halfpenny.   It is good to believe him.   If
he be not all that he pretendeth, *give,* and under
a personate father of a family, think (if thou
pleasest) that thou hast relieved an indigent
bachelor.   When they come with their counter-

s

feit looks, and mumping tones, think them players. You pay your money to see a comedian feign these things, which, concerning these poor people, thou canst not certainly tell whether they are feigned or not."

To the Shorter Catechist in Stevenson the beggar is not only a man demoralised, but a source of demoralisation in the persons whose benevolence he fraudulently exploits :

" The beggar lives by his knowledge of the average man.   He knows what he is about when he bandages his head, and hires and drugs a babe, and poisons life with *Poor Mary Ann* or *Long, Long Ago* ; he knows what he is about when he loads the critical ear and sickens the nice conscience with intolerable thanks ; they know what they are about, he and his crew, when they pervade the slums of cities, ghastly parodies of suffering, hateful parodies of gratitude.   This trade can scarce be called an imposition ; it has been so blown upon with exposures ; it flaunts its fraudulence so nakedly.   We pay them as we pay those who show us, in huge exaggeration, the monsters of our drinking-water ; or those who daily predict the fall of Britain.   We pay them for the pain they inflict, pay them, and wince, and hurry on.   And truly there is nothing that can shake the conscience like a beggar's thanks ; and that polity in which such protestations can be purchased for a shilling, seems no scene for an honest man."

Walter Raleigh says that Stevenson's " daintiness of diction is best seen in his earlier works." In his later works, and particularly in his fiction, his writing is more vigorous and direct, though it was " never unillumined by felicities that cause a thrill of pleasure to the reader." Miss Rebecca West wickedly suggests that, when Stevenson became a popular novelist, " the stay and breadwinner of Mr. Mudie," and realised the British public's dislike of all fineness of style, he deliberately played down to his audience. " He had," she says, " too prudent care to water down his gruel to suit sick England's stomach."

The author, like the actor, sometimes suffers from stage-fright. Walter Raleigh says :

" There is a kind of stage-fright that seizes on a man when he takes pen in hand to address an unknown body of hearers, no less than when he stands up to deliver himself to a sea of expectant faces. This is the true panic fear, that walks at mid-day, and unmans those whom it visits. Hence come reservations, qualifications, verbosity, and the see-saw of a wavering courage, which apes progress and purpose, as soldiers mark time with their feet. The writing produced under these auspices is of no greater moment than the incoherent loquacity of a nervous patient. All self-expression is a challenge thrown down to the world, to be taken up by whoso will ; and the spirit of timidity, when it touches a man, suborns him with the reminder that he holds his life and goods by the sufferance of his fellows. Thereupon he begins to doubt whether it is worth while to court a verdict of so grave possibilities, or to risk offending a judge whose customary geniality is merely the outcome of a fixed habit of inattention." [1]

But Stevenson was as little affected by his public as a professional writer can be. He, perhaps *malgré lui*, always gave them of his best.

Stevenson had a constant inclination to write his stories in the first person. He regarded this as a mere personal preference, but Mr. Percy Lubbock has pointed out that it was necessary for the plots that attracted him. Mr. Lubbock says :

" They were strongly romantic, vividly dramatic ; he never had occasion to use the first person for the effect I considered a while ago, its enhancement of a plain narrative. I called it the first step towards the dramatization of a story, and so it is in a book like *Esmond*, a broadly pictured novel of manners. But it is more than this in a book like *The Master of Ballantrae*, where the subject is a piece of forcible, closely knit action. The value of rendering it as somebody's narrative, of placing it in the mouth of a man who was there on the spot, is in this book the value of working the drama into a picture, of passing it through a man's thought and catching his reflection of it. As the

---

[1] *Style*, by Walter Raleigh, pp. 78, 79.

picture in *Esmond* is enhanced, so the drama in
Ballantrae is toned and qualified by the method of
presentation." [1]

In Stevenson, the man was greater than the
writer. It was indeed the mission of the writer
to reveal the man. Once more I quote Walter
Raleigh :

" A criticism of Stevenson is happy in this, that
from the writer it can pass with perfect trust and
perfect fluency to the man. He shares with
Goldsmith and Montaigne, his own favourite, the
happy privilege of making lovers among his
readers. ' To be the most beloved of English
writers—what a title that is for a man ! ' says
Thackeray of Goldsmith. In such matters, a dis-
pute for pre-eminence in the captivation of hearts
would be unseemly ; it is enough to say that
Stevenson too has his lovers among those who
have accompanied him on his *Inland Voyage*, or
through the fastnesses of the Cevennes in the wake
of Modestine. He is loved by those who never
saw his face." [2]

And Andrew Lang wrote : " When we consider the great variety of Stevenson's works, their
wide range, their tenderness, their sympathy,
their mastery of terror and pity, their gloom and
their gaiety ; when we remember that his sympathy and knowledge are as conspicuous in his

[1] *The Craft of Fiction*, by Percy Lubbock, p. 218.
[2] *Robert Louis Stevenson*, by Walter Raleigh, p. 78.

tales of the brown natives of the Pacific (*The Beach of Falesa*) as of Highlanders and Lowlanders, and the French of the fifteenth century; we can have little doubt concerning his place in literature." [1]

The craftsmanship of Stevenson's verse is far less supreme than that of his prose. William Archer said, in a typical Scottish phrase, that " verse was not his predestinate medium." He wrote verse indeed mainly as an amusement. It was the fashion of his time. All his friends wrote verse, and most of them, rather better than he. Mrs. Stevenson says : " Very few of my husband's poems were conceived with any other purpose than the entertainment of the moment." And in another place she wrote : " An itinerary of my husband's wanderings might almost be drawn from his collected poems." He sang as he tramped ! Perhaps the best thing ever said of Stevenson's poetry is Mr. Chesterton's wicked suggestion that " the best poetry of Miss Sitwell is after all a sort of parody of *A Child's Garden of Verses*, decked with slightly altered adjectives that would mildly surprise the child." [2]

As a matter of fact a good deal of the verse specially written for the child would mildly surprise the child when it did not bewilder him. Stevenson was a very sophisticated Peter Pan.

---

[1] *History of English Literature*, by Andrew Lang, p. 641.
[2] *Stevenson*, by G. K. Chesterton, p. 257.

No Scottish writer has ever been more essentially Scottish than Stevenson, and he was Scottish in his love of France. But had he been a Frenchman and not a Scot, he would have understood Villon, and would certainly not have been outraged by Zola. He was happy in Paris and in Fontainebleau. But most of the inhabitants of the Bohemia of Paris have always been foreigners, and to-day Montparnasse is almost a foreign quarter. Professor Sarolea says that " even as he sought the sunshine of the Riviera, even as he sought in French wisdom a release from an inhuman creed, so he sought the beauty and the chastening and mellowing discipline of French art." [1] He sought the sunshine of the Riviera because he was tubercular and could not live in Scotland. He was never released from a creed which was by no means entirely inhuman.

However much France may have affected Stevenson the artist, it affected the essentials of the man hardly at all. Professor Sarolea says : " The truth of the matter is that the philosophy of Stevenson is essentially the broad humanity of France. In a spiritual sense as well as in a literary sense the Scotch Jacobite is almost a French Jacobin and almost a French Liberal Catholic." [2] All this is an illusion. The philosophy of Stevenson is certainly not the broad humanity of France. Stevenson was not a Scottish Jacobite, but a Scot-

[1] *Stevenson and France* (Sarolea), p. 33. [2] *Ibid.*, pp. 15, 16.

tish Covenanter who wandered awhile from the fold, and he never was in the least like a French Jacobin or a French Liberal Catholic.

Professor Sarolea is mainly concerned to prove that Stevenson was the spiritual son of Montaigne. The Professor would have us believe first that the style of the French essayist is more attuned to Robert Louis Stevenson's mentality than the style of the great British essayists. The French, he says, are less dogmatic and less didactic. But what French writer was ever less dogmatic and less didactic than Charles Lamb? And Stevenson himself was certainly often both dogmatic and didactic.

Professor Sarolea suggests that Montaigne represents the anti-Calvinistic reaction of the sixteenth century, and that Stevenson represents the anti-Puritan reaction of the nineteenth. The first statement is perfectly true. Edward Dowden has said that Montaigne was three-fourths a pagan philosopher, and that the Christian in him "sailed in the car of the balloon." He was a nominal Catholic. He certainly rejected the Calvinistic doctrine of the vileness of man. But his philosophy involved a lively Protestant demand for the right of private judgment. There is, I admit, a real Stevensonian suggestion in Montaigne's statement, " I love life and cultivate it, such it has pleased God to bestow it upon us." But actually Stevenson was never content to accept any state of life as divinely arranged and therefore acceptable and unimprovable. He was always eager to climb to the stars. He always wanted to be on the side of the angels. The basic idea of Montaigne's philosophy is that we are what we are, and that we must make the best of it. For nature Montaigne has a regard as profound though not as fantastic as that of Rousseau. From nature a man may learn wisdom. " Prudence and the essence of wisdom is loyally to enjoy our being." Repentance—and here, of course, he is at issue with Catholics even more than with Protestants—is absurd. " Be pleased to excuse what I often say," he wrote, " that I rarely repent and that my conscience is satisfied with itself not as the conscience of an angel or a horse, but as the conscience of a man ! " And to this he added :

" The saying that repentance immediately follows the sin seems not to have respect to sin in its high estate, which is lodged in us as in its own proper habitation. One may disown and retract the vices that surprise us, and to which we are hurried by passions ; but those which by a long habit are rooted in a strong and vigorous will are not subject to contradiction. Repentance is no other but a recanting of the will and an opposition to our fancies, which lead us which way they please. It makes this person disown his former virtue and continency."

And Edward Dowden has said :

" He found it very hard to imagine any sudden

change of heart or life. He could conceive a desire for a complete alteration or reformation of his being, but this was no more repentance, he says, than if he were dissatisfied because he was not an angel or Cato. On the whole he could do no better than he had done ; in the same circumstances he would again act as he had acted ; it may be that he was stained throughout with a universal tincture, but there were no definite spots ; if he were to repent at all, it must not be a particular, but a universal repentance, and he was well pleased to be a man. True, he had now and again erred seriously, but this was not through lack of prudent deliberation ; it was rather through want of good luck ; the events could not have been other than they were ; they belonged to the large course of the universe, to the entire enchainment of Stoical causes. Certainly the voice that speaks to us is not the voice of St. Augustine, nor the voice of St. Paul." [1]

Nor is it the voice of Stevenson. But it is the voice of Rabelais, and it might be the voice of Charles Lamb, who " would have been," said Thomas Hood, " (if the foundation had existed, save in the fiction of Rabelais), of the Utopian order of Thelemites, where each man under Scriptural warrant did what seemed good in his own eyes." [2]   In none of his writings, not even in

---

[1] *Montaigne*, by Edward Dowden, p. 281.
[2] *Life of Charles Lamb*, by E. V. Lucas, vol. ii. p. 56.

the days when he was most in revolt against the dour Puritanism of his home and his native country, is there any real suggestion of Montaigne's amiable paganism in Stevenson.

In stark contrast to Montaigne, Stevenson was constantly professing repentance and the need of repentance, and so insistently did he feel the need that, in the manner of the Salvation Army convert, he took pleasure in exaggerating youthful wickedness. Stevenson wrote in *Crabbed Age and Youth* : " If a man live to any considerable age, it cannot be denied that he laments his imprudences." Montaigne lamented nothing but ill fortune. Stevenson wrote in *The Amateur Emigrant* : " You cannot run away from a weakness ; you must some time fight it out or perish." Montaigne would have said that as you cannot run away from a weakness, you had better enjoy it.

Professor Sarolea suggests that Stevenson was obliged to disguise his real sentiments for fear of hurting his father, and in later years of antagonising his public. Certainly his occasional outbursts against his public hint at revolt against the necessity of pleasing it. He wrote to Gosse in 1886 : " Let us tell each other sad stories of the bestiality of the beast whom we feed. What he likes is the newspaper ; and to me the press is the mouth of a sewer, where lying is professed as from an university chair, and everything prurient, and ignoble, and essentially dull, finds its abode and pulpit. I do not like mankind ; but men, and not all of these—and fewer women. As for respecting the race, and, above all, that fatuous rabble of burgesses called ' the public,' God save me from such irreligion !—that way lies disgrace and dishonour. There must be something wrong in me, or I would not be popular." But too much significance can easily be attached to such an ourburst. For the most part, when Stevenson was pleasing his public he was pleasing himself. And even though Stevenson might jeer at his public, it was none the less his business to give it his best. He says in *Lay Morals* :

" Every piece of work which is not as good as you can make it, which you have palmed off imperfect, meagrely thought, niggardly in execution, upon mankind, who is your paymaster on parole, and in a sense your pupil, every hasty or slovenly or untrue performance, should rise up against you in the court of your own heart and condemn you for a thief."

Professor Sarolea thinks that Stevenson " is often compelled to disguise his deeper meaning." But Henley complained that he was always seeking pretexts for " highly moral deliverances." Montaigne said of himself : " I do not teach, I only relate." Stevenson might have said : " I relate in order that I may preach."

To him life was a gallant adventure, but a man's life was beset with duties that must be honourably fulfilled. He wrote in *Notes on Edinburgh* : " So long as men do their duty, even if it be greatly in a misapprehension, they will be leading pattern lives ; and whether or not they come to lie beside a martyrs' monument, we may be sure they will find a safe haven somewhere in the providence of God."

Man must expect failure and profit from it. " Faith counts certainly on failure," he says in *Virginibus Puerisque*, " and takes honourable defeat to be a form of victory." Indeed, however, he may strive and however worthy may be his intentions, there will be for every man the constant need of repentance and forgiveness. This is expressed in the prayers written for the household at Vailima :

" Help us, at the same time, with the grace of courage, that we be none of us cast down when we sit lamenting amid the ruins of our happiness or our integrity ; touch us with fire from the altar, that we may be up and doing to rebuild our city.

" We beseech Thee, Lord, to behold us with favour, folk of many families and nations, gathered together in the peace of this roof ; weak men and women, subsisting under the covert of Thy patience. Be patient still ; suffer us yet a while longer—with our broken purposes of good, with our idle endeavours against evil, suffer us a while longer to endure, and (if it may be) help us to do better."

Man is born in sin and shapen in iniquity. In the essay *Pulvis et Umbra*, published in *Scribner's Magazine* in 1888, Stevenson wrote :

"What a monstrous spectre is this man, the disease of the agglutinated dust, lifting alternate feet or lying drugged with slumber ; killing, feeding, growing, bringing forth small copies of himself ; grown upon with hair like grass, fitted with eyes that move and glitter in his face ; a thing to set children screaming ;—and yet looked at nearlier, known as his fellows know him, how surprising are his attributes ! Poor soul, here for so little, cast among so many hardships, filled with desires so incommensurate and so inconsistent, savagely surrounded, savagely descended, irremediably condemned to prey upon his fellow lives ; who should have blamed him had he been of a piece with his destiny and a being merely barbarous ? And we look and behold him instead filled with imperfect virtues : infinitely childish, often admirably valiant, often touchingly kind ; sitting down, amidst his momentary life, to debate of right and wrong and the attributes of the deity ; rising up to do battle for an egg or die for an idea ; singling out his friends and his mate with cordial affection ; bringing forth in pain, rearing with long-suffering solicitude, his young."

William Archer has called this essay Stevenson's "loftiest and austerest utterance." "It tingles," he says, " with realisation of the mystery of the universe." Certainly the passage that I have quoted tingles with the Puritan notion of the nature of man. I suggest two comparisons. " Man in his birth is compared to an Ass (an unclean Beast)," Bunyan wrote in *The Life and Death of Mr. Badman.* Richard Baxter warned his wife : " The best creature-affections have a mixture of some creature-imperfections, and therefore need some gall to wean us from the faulty part. God must be known to be God, our rest, and therefore the best creature to be but a creature ! O miserable world (how long must I continue in it ? And why is this wretched heart so loath to leave it) where we can have no fire without smoak, and our dearest friends must be our greatest grief, and when we begin in hope, and love, and joy, before we are aware, we fall into an answerable measure of distress. Learn by experience, when any condition is inordinately or excessively sweet to thee, to say, *From hence must be my sorrow.* (O how true !) " [1]

To Stevenson the heart of the mystery is that man, " the disease of the agglutinated dust," a phrase that might well excite Mr. Benson's scorn, still possesses splendid virtues. He was, as Mr. Chesterton has said, " continually bearing witness to the Fall," but he could not altogether ignore

[1] *Richard Baxter and Margaret Charlton,* by J. T. Wilkinson, p. 105.

the evidences of the Resurrection.   He goes on in
Pulvis et Umbra :

" To touch the heart of his mystery, we find in
him one thought, strange to the point of lunacy :
the thought of duty ; the thought of something
owing to himself, to his neighbour, to his God :
an ideal of decency, to which he would rise if it
were possible ; a limit of shame, below which, if
it be possible, he will not stoop.   The design in
most men is one of conformity ; here and there,
in picked natures, it transcends itself and soars on
the other side, arming martyrs with independence ;
but in all, in their degrees, it is a bosom of thought.
. . . But in man, at least, it sways with so complete an empire that merely selfish things come
second, even with the selfish : that appetites are
starved, fears are conquered, pains supported ;
that almost the dullest shrinks from the reproof of
a glance, although it were a child's ; and all but
the most cowardly stand amid the risks of war ;
and the more noble, having strongly conceived
an act as due to their ideal, affront and embrace
death."

When he wrote the essay—his mood often
changed—he wrote as one with little hope. "Man
is indeed marked for failure in his efforts to do
right."   Therefore, say Montaigne and Samuel
Butler and Ibsen and Mr. Shaw, let him be content to be himself.   But Stevenson perceives that,
however certain the failure, the striving will con-

tinue. Man will go on searching for the Holy Grail. "Surely," he says, "we should find it both touching and inspiriting, that in a field from which success is banished, our race should not cease from labour." And labour is God inspired and is not altogether vanity : "And as we dwell, we living things, in our isle of terror and under the imminent hand of death, God forbid it should be man the erected, the reasoner, the wise in his own eyes—God forbid it should be man that wearies in well-doing, that despairs of unrewarded effort, or utters the language of complaint. Let it be enough for faith, that the whole creation groans in mortal frailty, strives with unconquerable constancy : surely not all in vain."

Courage he esteemed as the greatest of the virtues—he came of a courageous race—and courage is, among other things, "the constancy to endure oneself." Montaigne enjoyed himself. So does Mr. Chesterton. But unless Stevenson was hopelessly insincere, he often suffered from the common self-loathing of the Puritan, and this may be partly traced, but not entirely, to his ill-health. I do not believe that Stevenson was insincere though he was sometimes unctuous, as in the final sentence of *The Morality of the Profession of Letters* : "For surely at this time of the day in the nineteenth century, there is nothing that an honest man should fear more timorously than

getting and spending more than he deserves."
And unctuousness is a Puritan failing.

The circumstances of his life made him regard
life as primarily a fight, and he was a brave and
not unhappy warrior. He wrote to George
Meredith :

" For fourteen years I have not had a day's real
health ; I have wakened sick and gone to bed
weary ; and I have done my work unflinchingly.
I have written in bed, and written out of it,
written in hemorrhages written in sickness,
written torn by coughing, written when my head
swam for weakness ; and for so long, it seems to
me I have won my wager and recovered my glove.
I am better now, have been, rightly speaking,
since I first came to the Pacific ; and still, few are
the days when I am not in some physical distress.
And the battle goes on—ill or well, is a trifle ;
so as it goes. I was made for a contest, and the
Powers have so willed that my battlefield should
be this dingy, inglorious one of the bed and the
physic bottle."

" Stevenson," says Mr. Lloyd Osbourne,
" hated materialism." Living in an age still
influenced by Matthew Arnold, he associated
materialism with the middle classes : " He judged
it to be the supreme danger and curse of our
civilisation—that comfortable, well-fed, compla-
cent materialism against which he was always
railing. No Socialist ever used the word ' bour-

geoisic' with more contempt than he. He thought that the lower classes and the higher could alike be fired by high ideals, but that the mass of the middle class was almost hopelessly antagonistic to human advancement. Its un-reasoning self-satisfaction, its exploitation of the helpless, its hypocritical morality, its oppression of women, its intolerable attitude towards art and literature, were all to him a series of inexcusable offences." [1]

Despite the absurdly exaggerated dissolute years in Edinburgh, and the Bohemianism of Paris and Fontainebleau, Stevenson was almost entirely uninterested in the problem of sex, and here he had none of the not uncommon morbid preoccupation of the sick and impotent. So far as sex is concerned, Stevenson was as pernickety a Puritan as Dean Inge and Mr. Shaw, and he had almost as complete an ignorance of the part passion plays in ordinary life as Mr. Shaw. He was revolted by Zola, though, as Sir Edmund Gosse has recorded, Zola could, on occasion, write Stevensonian stories :

" In 1883, Zola published a third volume of short stories, under the title of the opening one, *Le Capitaine Burle*. This collection contains the delicate series of brief semi-autobiographical essays called *Aux Champs*, little studies of past impression, touched with a charm which is almost

[1] *New Arabian Nights*, Introd., p. xv.

kindred to that of Robert Louis Stevenson's memories." [1]

The loss, too, of his admiration for Balzac may be traced to the Puritanism in his blood. The critic may have grown bored, for Anatole France admits that Balzac's thought is sometimes heavy and his style sometimes dull. But it was the Balzac world that outraged the fastidious. The pious long-haired sculptor of Anatole's sketch denounced Balzac as the Lucifer of Literature. How could the Shorter Catechist tolerate the Lucifer of Literature ?

M. Louis Cazamian has noted that Stevenson's temperament at bottom is " almost Puritanic," and the suggestion contradicts Professor Sarolea. M. Cazamian writes :

" Without any explicit profession, Stevenson gives his adhesion to anti-intellectualism, the need of which he experiences, like many others about him. His novels, his poems, his critical studies or essays, have their unity there. The first minister to wonder and the passion for dramatic adventure ; the second subtly enter into the unsophisticated emotions of the young ; the third analyse authors, their writings, or the wisdom which we learn from reflection, with a simplicity which goes straight to direct data, to those which the intelligence will readily neglect or despise. In this sense, he always wrote *Virginibus Puerisque* ;

[1] *French Profiles*, by Edmund Gosse, p. 140.

and his artistic aim was to reconcile the scrupulous refinement of maturity with the youthful purity of the theme." [1]

Stevenson was indeed "clean" in the Victorian sense. One would have dearly loved to have read a review of *Point Counter Point* from his pen, and Sir Edmund Gosse very acutely noted that " it was the real Stevenson who once said : ' I think it is always wholesome to read Leslie Stephen.' "

A man, always in danger of dying, can never think normally, though he may think bravely and wisely, of death. St. Paul died daily. Stevenson nearly died daily. The majority of men think very little of death, and regard all the world as mortal except themselves. To the man harassed by ill-health, even though at his best he may with easy humour enjoy his ill-health, death is the deliverer. I have already quoted some of Stevenson's references to death. In the following verse he is optimist rather than orthodox Christian :

> The look of Death is both severe and mild,
> And all the words of Death are grave and sweet ;
> He holds ajar the door of his retreat ;
> The hermitage of life, it may be styled ;
> He pardons sinners, cleanses the defiled,
> And comfortably welcomes weary feet.
> The look of Death is both severe and mild,
> And all the words of Death are grave and sweet.

---

[1] *A History of English Literature,* by Émile Legouis and Louis Cazamian, vol. ii. p. 439.

Compare this with Gilbert's expression of comfortable nineteenth-century materialism :

> Is life a boon ?
>> If so, it must befall
>> That Death, whene'er he call,
> Must call too soon.
>> Though fourscore years he give,
>> Yet one would pray to live
> Another moon !

Often doubting, often bewildered, Stevenson was a man of faith.   Life was hard.   Failure was certain.   But man created in the image of his Maker was assured of final victory.   " The best that is in us is better than we can understand."

CHAPTER XIII

FANNY STEVENSON

THE lover is a bad judge of his lady's beauty. But Stevenson's description of his wife is no more ecstatic than that of Edmund Gosse, who said of her : " She is dark and rich hearted like some wonderful wine-red jewel."

It was once said that every beautiful thing given to the world by genius was born of a man and a woman, and it might have been added that it was generally born out of wedlock. How much the creative artist owes to the women with whom he has been most intimately associated is a problem of genuine human interest. And while, of course, it is true that it is Mary who chooses the better part, Martha, who secures the little comforts, protects against the little irritations, and provides an atmosphere of peace and perhaps of adulation—few men with genius or without ever weary of being adored—has played her great part in making smooth the path of the singer of songs and the teller of tales.

The debt of most men of conspicuous gifts to their wives must remain a matter of speculation, but there is no doubt whatever of the heavy debt

that Stevenson owed to Mrs. Stevenson. Without her he would have died years before he did,
and without her sedulous care, ceaseless en-
couragement, and considerable critical faculty,
his achievement would have been far less, and he
would probably have merely been remembered
as a writer of a few volumes of suggestive essays,
and a little verse of no great quality. Her sister
has written : " But above and beyond his wife's
care for his physical well-being was the strong
courage with which she stood by him in his hours
of gloom and heartened him up to the fight. Her
profound faith in his genius before the rest of the
world had come to recognize it had a great deal
to do with keeping up his faith in himself, and her
discriminating taste in literature was such that he
had begun even then to submit all his writings to
her criticism." [1]

There is indeed no exaggeration in Miss Rosaline Masson's statement, perfervid as it may
appear : " All that Louis Stevenson is to-day, to
thousands who never knew him in the flesh, to
whom his memory is not only tender and lovable
and brilliant, but is held in reverence and earnestness ; to whom his writings, the delight of them,
the message they give ; his life and the lessons it
teaches ; all that ' R. L. S.' stands for to-day, and
that the word ' Stevensonian ' awakes in brother-
liness and sympathy between those who are

[1] *Life of Mrs. R. L. Stevenson*, by N. V. de G. Sanchez, pp. 65, 66.

divided by ' mountains and a waste of seas,'—all this is accorded to the Robert Louis Stevenson that he became, to the Robert Louis Stevenson that died fourteen years after his marriage." [1]

Few women, distinguished or undistinguished, have ever succeeded in conquering their " in-laws," and Thomas Stevenson, the dour, Calvin-istic Scot, could not have been an easy man to conquer. But at once he appreciated the quali-ties of his daughter-in-law, and between her and him there began a very complete understanding friendship. His pet name for her was a " besom," which, being translated, means a managing per-son, which she assuredly had to be. He trusted her judgment, he grew more and more satisfied that his son should be in her hands, and Steven-son himself said that he had never seen his father so completely subjugated. She had a comple-mentary admiration. She said in a letter to her mother-in-law : " What a Christmas of thanks-giving this should be for us all, with Louis so well, his father so well, everything pointing to comfort and happiness. Louis is making such a success with his work, and doing better work every day. Dear mother and father of my beloved husband, I send you Christmas greetings from my heart of hearts. I mean to have a Merry Christmas and be as glad and thankful as possible for all the un-deserved mercies and blessings that have been

[1] *Life of Robert Louis Stevenson,* by Rosaline Masson, p. 193.

showered me." [1] As for Stevenson's mother,
Lady Balfour has said: "It is a testimonial both to
her (Louis's wife) and to Mrs. Thomas Stevenson
that though they were as the poles apart in character, yet each loved and appreciated the other
most fully."

Edmund Gosse has written of his friend's wife
as " a charming lady whom we all learned to regard as the most appropriate and helpful companion that Louis could possibly have secured."
Sidney Colvin has said : " Parents and friends—
if it is permissible to one of the latter to say as
much—rejoiced to recognize in Stevenson's wife
a character as strong, interesting, and romantic
almost as his own ; an inseparable sharer of all
his thoughts, and staunch companion of all his
adventures ; the most open-hearted of friends to
all who loved him ; the most shrewd and stimulating critic of his work ; and in sickness, despite
her own precarious health, the most devoted and
most efficient of nurses." [2]

" All my life I have taken care of others," Mrs.
Stevenson wrote to Mr. Scribner at the end of her
life in 1913, " and yet I have always wanted to be
taken care of, for naturally I belong to the clinging vine sort of woman." She was an old woman
when she wrote that, and the great romance of
her life had finished nearly twenty years before,

[1] *Life of Mrs. R. L. Stevenson*, by N. V. de G. Sanchez, p. 109.
[2] *Life of R. L. Stevenson*, by Rosaline Masson, p. 198.

and there is, indeed, much more suggestion of the masterful woman than of the clinging woman in the incidents of her life with her second husband. Equally evident is the fact that her service to him entailed ceaseless self-sacrifice. What one of her friends described as her " robust inconsequential philosophy of life " enabled her to endure discomfort with a measure of equanimity. Living at a high altitude made her ill ; nevertheless she went happily to Davos. She was a Californian and loved sunshine, and Swiss winters were purgatory to her. She wrote to her mother-in-law : " I cannot deny that living here is like living in a well of desolation. Sometimes I feel quite frantic to look out somewhere, and almost as though I should suffocate. But may Davos forgive me ! It has done so much for Louis that I am ashamed to say anything against it." [1]

It was evidently depressing to live on a mountain top surrounded by tubercular patients, but there were certain compensations : " It is depressing to live with dying and suffering people all about you, but a sanatorium develops a great deal of human interest and sympathy. Every one knows what the other should do, and each among the patients helps to look after the rest. The path of duty always lies so plain before other people's feet." [2]

[1] *Life of Mrs. R. L. Stevenson*, by N. V. de G. Sanchez, p. 91.
[2] *Ibid.*, p. 89.

She was an extremely bad sailor and hated the sea. " I hate the sea and am afraid of it," she wrote, " though no one will believe that because in time of danger I do not make an outcry." Nevertheless she went for cruise after cruise in the Pacific.

The years of wandering in the South Seas before they settled at Vailima were for Mrs. Stevenson filled with trying and insistent responsibilities. It was she who made all the preparations for the voyages. It was she who had to take constant care for the comfort of the sick man. As her sister said, " she cheerfully endured a thousand discomforts, hardships, and even dangers for the sake of the slight increase of health and happiness to the life of the loved one."

With some bright intervals, there was hardly a week in her married life when death was not, as it were, standing menacingly outside her window, and the wear and tear of using every subtle means for preventing him from stealing away the man she loved must have been intensely wearying. " Fanny is much out of sorts, principally through perpetual misery for me," Stevenson once wrote to his father. But the perpetual misery—which could be written more truthfully, perpetual anxiety—was the ceaseless accompaniment of joy and pride.

In her biography of her sister, Mrs. Sanchez has quoted freely from a diary which Mrs. Steven-

son kept from her arrival at Vailima until her
husband's death, and here in Samoa her days
were certainly sufficiently well filled. She was
often ill, and in the early days domestic matters
were constantly in a turmoil. On one occasion
Louis wished to go down to Apia :

" It took all six of the boys to catch the pony,
and in the meantime Louis was having a desperate struggle to find his clothes and dress. I was
in a dazed state with fever and quinine and could
not help him at all. At last he got away, in what
sort of garb I tremble to think, and he was hardly
out of sight before I discovered all the things
he had been in search of—in their right places
naturally." [1]

Hurricanes were the fashion, earthquakes were
not infrequent, and " each night has its separate
plague of insects." These, of course, were early
days, and afterwards life at Vailima approached
the luxurious. But there were constant servant
troubles and, as Stevenson developed into a sort
of patriarch, his wife was in constant demand
as an adviser and sometimes as a nurse. Mrs.
Sanchez quotes a letter of her sister's :

" Socially," she writes, " Samoa was not dull.
There were many entertainments given by diplo-
mats and officials in Apia. Besides native feasts
there were afternoon teas, evening receptions,
dinner parties, private and public balls, paper

[1] *Life of Mrs. R. L. Stevenson*, by N. V. de G. Sanchez, p. 179.

chases on horseback, polo, tennis parties, and
picnics. Sometimes a party of flower-wreathed
natives might come dancing over the lawn at
Vailima, or a band of sailors from a man-of-war
would be seen gathered in an embarrassed knot
at the front gate." [1]

It is easy to understand how much Mrs. Stevenson gave to her husband. No man can tell what
he gave to her. As I have suggested before, he
was a receiver rather than a giver, but he certainly gave to her far more than he gave to any
other of his friends, and his gratitude and understanding were her sufficient reward. His little
affectation in addressing her as " my dear fellow "
suggests the measure of comradeship that existed
between them, and there is ample evidence in
Mr. Lloyd Osbourne's invaluable biographical
notes of his appreciation of her critical acumen.
There is a pretty dedication to her of some
of his verses that no woman could fail to appreciate :

> My first gift and my last, to you
> I dedicate this fascicle of songs—
> The only wealth I have :
> Just as they are, to you.
>
> I speak the truth in soberness, and say
> I had rather bring a light to your clear eyes,
> Had rather hear you praise
> This bosomful of songs.

---

[1] *Life of Mrs. R. L. Stevenson,* by N. V. de G. Sanchez, pp. 200-01.

To him she was the most beautiful woman in the world. To her, he was the greatest of geniuses and the greatest of heroes. She wrote to her mother-in-law : " I suppose you are even prouder of Louis than I am, for he is only mine accidentally, and he is yours by birth and blood. Two or three times last night I woke up just from pure pleasure to think of all the people I know reading about Louis." [1] And in another letter : " I should be perfectly appalled if I were asked to exchange his faults for other people's virtues." [2]

Though she lived for years after his death, her life remained tragically empty. " The years ahead of me," she wrote to her daughter, " seem like large empty rooms with high ceilings and echoes. Not gay, say you, but I was never one for gaiety much and I may discover a certain grandeur in the emptiness." [3]

After Stevenson's death, Henry James wrote to his wife : " To have lived in the light of that splendid life, that beautiful, bountiful being—only to see it, from one moment to the other, converted into a fable as strange and romantic as one of his own, a thing that has been and has ended, is an anguish into which no one can enter with you fully, and of which no one can drain the cup for you. You are nearest to the pain because you

[1] *Life of Mrs. R. L. Stevenson*, by N. V. de G. Sanchez, p. 105.
[2] *Ibid.*, p. 117.   [3] *Ibid.*, p. 263.

were nearest to the joy and the pride. . . . When I think of your own situation I fall into a mere confusion of pity and wonder, with the sole sense of your being as brave a spirit as he was (all of whose bravery you shared) to hold on by." [1]

When her husband was buried, Mrs. Stevenson stayed for a few months in Vailima, and then went back to her native California, returning to Samoa in the autumn of 1895, after a short stay in Honolulu. "Everything here," she wrote to her mother-in-law, "reminds me of Louis, and I do not think there is one moment that I am not thinking of him. People say : 'What a comfort his great name must be to you !' It is a pride to me, but not a comfort ; I would rather have my Louis here with me, poor and unknown." [2]

Mrs. Stevenson stopped at Vailima until 1898. Then the death of her mother-in-law, the claims of her son and daughter, and her own ill-health, compelled her to sell the house to a Russian merchant—it afterwards became the official residence of the German Governor of the island—and return to England where, among other things, she made arrangements for the writing of her husband's biography by his cousin, Graham Balfour. She spent the winter of 1898 in Madeira, and then returned to California. But the *wanderlust* re-

---

[1] *Life of Mrs. R. L. Stevenson*, by N. V. de G. Sanchez, pp. 223-4.
[2] *Ibid.*, p. 228.

mained with her, and the later years saw travels in Mexico and trips to Europe. She was in San Francisco in 1906 at the time of the great earthquake. Her last days were spent in a beautiful house at Santa Barbara. She died on February 18th, 1914. Lady Balfour has said of her :

" I don't think I ever knew a woman who was a more perfect 'gentleman.' Scorning all that was not direct, and true, and simple, she herself hated disguise or casuistry in any form. Her eyes looked through your soul and out at the other side, but you never felt that her judgment, whatever it was, would be harsh. She was curiously detached, and yet you always wanted her sympathy, and if she loved you it never failed you. She was a strong partisan, which was perhaps the most feminine part of her character. She was wholly un-English, but she made allowances for every English tradition. My English maids loved her without understanding her in the least. I never knew any one that had such a way as she had of turning your little vagaries and habits and fads to your notice with their funny side out, so that all the time you were subtly flattered and secretly delighted." [1]

In the spring of 1915, her daughter carried her ashes to Samoa, and they were placed in her husband's mountain tomb. With the bronze tablet

[1] *Life of Mrs. R. L. Stevenson,* by N. V. de G. Sanchez, pp. 318-19.

on which *Requiem* is written, is another inscribed
with Stevenson's verse :

> Teacher, tender, comrade, wife,
> A fellow-farer true through life,
> Heart-whole and soul-free,
> The August Father gave to me.